T0194691

MACAT

An Analysis of

Christopher R. Browning's

Ordinary Men
Reserve Police Batallion 101 and the Final Solution in Poland

Tom Stammers

Published by Macat International Ltd
24:13 Coda Centre, 189 Munster Road, London SW6 6AW.

Distributed exclusively by Routledge
2 Park Square, Milton Park, Abingdon, Oxon OX14 4RN
711 Third Avenue, New York, NY 10017, USA

Routledge is an imprint of the Taylor & Francis Group, an informa business

www.macat.com
info@macat.com

Cataloguing in Publication Data
A catalogue record for this book is available from the British Library.
Library of Congress Cataloguing-in-Publication Data is available upon request.
Cover illustration: Etienne Gilfillan

ISBN 978-1-912302-45-1 (hardback)
ISBN 978-1-912127-47-4 (paperback)
ISBN 978-1-912281-33-6 (e-book)

Notice

CONTENTS

THE MACAT LIBRARY

The Macat Library is a series of unique academic explorations of seminal works in the humanities and social sciences – books and papers that have had a significant and widely recognised impact on their disciplines. It has been created to serve as much more than just a summary of what lies between the covers of a great book. It illuminates and explores the influences on, ideas of, and impact of that book. Our goal is to offer a learning resource that encourages critical thinking and fosters a better, deeper understanding of important ideas.

Each publication is divided into three Sections: Influences, Ideas, and Impact. Each Section has four Modules. These explore every important facet of the work, and the responses to it.

This Section-Module structure makes a Macat Library book easy to use, but it has another important feature. Because each Macat book is written to the same format, it is possible (and encouraged!) to cross-reference multiple Macat books along the same lines of inquiry or research. This allows the reader to open up interesting interdisciplinary pathways.

To further aid your reading, lists of glossary terms and people mentioned are included at the end of this book (these are indicated by an asterisk [*] throughout) – as well as a list of works cited.

Macat has worked with the University of Cambridge to identify the elements of critical thinking and understand the ways in which six different skills combine to enable effective thinking.
Three allow us to fully understand a problem; three more give us the tools to solve it. Together, these six skills make up the **PACIER** model of critical thinking. They are:

ANALYSIS – understanding how an argument is built
EVALUATION – exploring the strengths and weaknesses of an argument
INTERPRETATION – understanding issues of meaning

CREATIVE THINKING – coming up with new ideas and fresh connections
PROBLEM-SOLVING – producing strong solutions
REASONING – creating strong arguments

To find out more, visit **WWW.MACAT.COM.**

CRITICAL THINKING AND *ORDINARY MEN*

Primary critical thinking skill: EVALUATION
Secondary critical thinking skill: INTERPRETATION

Of all the controversies facing historians today, few are more divisive or more important than the question of how and why the Holocaust occurred.

What led thousands of Germans – many of them middle-aged reservists with little Nazi zeal – to willingly commit acts of genocide? Was it ideology? Was there something rotten in the German soul? Or was it – as Christopher Browning argues in this highly influential book – more a matter of conformity, a response to intolerable social and psychological pressure?

Ordinary Men is a microhistory, the detailed study of a single unit in the Nazi killing machine. Browning evaluates a wide range of evidence to seek to explain the actions of the "ordinary men" who made up reserve Police Battalion 101, taking advantage of the wide range of resources prepared in the early 1960s for a proposed war crimes trial. He concludes that his subjects were not "evil"; rather, their actions are best explained by a desire to be part of a team – and hence not to shirk responsibility that would otherwise fall on the shoulders of comrades – together with a readiness to obey authority.

Browning's ability to evaluate the strengths and weaknesses of arguments – both the survivors' and those advanced by other historians – is what sets his work apart from other studies that have attempted to get to the root of the motivations for the Holocaust, and it is also what marks *Ordinary Men* as one of the most important works of its generation.

ABOUT THE AUTHOR OF THE ORIGINAL WORK

American historian **Christopher Browning** was born in 1944. His academic career had not received widespread attention until the 1992 publication of *Ordinary Men*, but this book caused a stir—particularly in relation to another work on the Holocaust by Daniel Goldhagen, at the time a forthright Harvard academic. Their vastly differing opinions about the Nazis and their killing, and the subsequent public debate, drew worldwide attention. Browning's views were commonly seen as more credible, and he is now regarded as the foremost American historian of the Holocaust.

ABOUT THE AUTHORS OF THE ANALYSIS

Dr Thomas Stammers is lecturer in Modern European history at Durham University, where he specialises in the cultural history of France in the age of revolution. He is the author of *Collection, Recollection, Revolution: Scavenging the Past in Nineteenth-Century Paris*. Dr Stammers's research interests include a wide range of historiographical and theoretical controversies related to the history of modern Europe.

ABOUT MACAT

GREAT WORKS FOR CRITICAL THINKING

Macat is focused on making the ideas of the world's great thinkers accessible and comprehensible to everybody, everywhere, in ways that promote the development of enhanced critical thinking skills.

It works with leading academics from the world's top universities to produce new analyses that focus on the ideas and the impact of the most influential works ever written across a wide variety of academic disciplines. Each of the works that sit at the heart of its growing library is an enduring example of great thinking. But by setting them in context – and looking at the influences that shaped their authors, as well as the responses they provoked – Macat encourages readers to look at these classics and game-changers with fresh eyes. Readers learn to think, engage and challenge their ideas, rather than simply accepting them.

'Macat offers an amazing first-of-its-kind tool for interdisciplinary learning and research. Its focus on works that transformed their disciplines and its rigorous approach, drawing on the world's leading experts and educational institutions, opens up a world-class education to anyone.'

Andreas Schleicher
Director for Education and Skills, Organisation for Economic Co-operation and Development

'Macat is taking on some of the major challenges in university education ... They have drawn together a strong team of active academics who are producing teaching materials that are novel in the breadth of their approach.'

Prof Lord Broers,
former Vice-Chancellor of the University of Cambridge

'The Macat vision is exceptionally exciting. It focuses upon new modes of learning which analyse and explain seminal texts which have profoundly influenced world thinking and so social and economic development. It promotes the kind of critical thinking which is essential for any society and economy. This is the learning of the future.'

Rt Hon Charles Clarke, former UK Secretary of State for Education

'The Macat analyses provide immediate access to the critical conversation surrounding the books that have shaped their respective discipline, which will make them an invaluable resource to all of those, students and teachers, working in the field.'

Professor William Tronzo, University of California at San Diego

WAYS IN TO THE TEXT

KEY POINTS

- Christopher Browning is an internationally respected historian of the Holocaust.*
- *Ordinary Men* changed the way the Holocaust is studied.
- *Ordinary Men* was the first work to try to explore the Holocaust through the eyes of its perpetrators.

Who Is Christopher Browning?

Christopher Browning is the leading American historian of the Holocaust. He was born in Chicago in 1944, and as a young man he was profoundly marked by the turbulent events of the 1960s and 1970s. The country was divided: first over the Civil Rights Movement,* then over reactions to the violence—and atrocities—of the Vietnam War.* Then in the early 1970s came revelations of political corruption during the presidency of Richard Nixon.* These events made Browning question *why* people commit terrible crimes. And this led him to study the Holocaust.

Browning's early research looked at the role of government officials, the bureaucrats who had formulated Nazi* policy in Eastern Europe. He then went on to study the men who had carried out these policies. Indeed, this was the topic of *Ordinary Men: Reserve Police Battalion 101 and the Final Solution in Poland*, Browning's vivid and harrowing account of a German police force in an occupied country.

The book became a landmark study in the history of the Holocaust, asking the question, "How could seemingly unexceptional men become hardened killers?" It won Browning—who had been teaching at a private university in the state of Washington since 1974—a prestigious professorship at the University of North Carolina at Chapel Hill.

Throughout his career Browning had the same goal, to clarify how the Holocaust happened and what it meant. His work led to his involvement in the public sphere, and he appeared as a key witness in the famous trial of the English Holocaust denier David Irving.* He has worked with Yad Vashem,* the museum of the Holocaust in Jerusalem, and he continues to write acclaimed books. Some have been macro-level views of the Holocaust, examining how the policy to exterminate the Jews* actually emerged. Others are micro-scale case histories, exploring the experiences of both perpetrators and victims.

What Does *Ordinary Men* Say?

Published in 1992, *Ordinary Men* is a book about the behavior and psychology of 500 German men during World War II.* The men of Reserve Police Battalion 101* were policemen, not soldiers. Posted to Nazi-occupied Poland, the tasks they were assigned included guarding trains and rounding Jews up into ghettos.* But they were also involved in the massacre of unarmed men, women, and children. The question at the heart of *Ordinary Men* is, "Why did these men do such things?"

In an early review of the book the British historian Ian Kershaw* predicted that it would become a classic. So it proved. A second edition appeared in 1998 and a third, British edition was issued in 2001.

There are a number of reasons why *Ordinary Men* had such an impact. Before it was published academics had become locked in a debate about *why* the Holocaust had happened. Intentionalists* said it was because Hitler* had always intended to eliminate the Jews. When his chance came, he took it. Functionalists* said that the Holocaust happened as a result of bureaucratic decisions and the way the war unfolded. However, *Ordinary Men* asked new questions and as a result helped to move the debate on.

Browning changed *who* academics studied. Prior to *Ordinary Men* the academic focus had been on a narrow elite of Nazi planners. Following the book, historians began to research other social groups.

In the 1960s the State Prosecutor in Hamburg had ordered an investigation into the men of Reserve Police Battalion 101, among others. In all, 210 men were interrogated, giving surprisingly frank and often distressing testimony about their time in Poland. Although the legal case against these men stalled, Browning used the judicial records to produce his own microhistory* of this battalion. It changed the way the Holocaust was seen. The Final Solution* had always been associated with concentration camps* and killing on an industrial scale. Browning's work though showed that millions had died as the result of face-to-face killing by specially drafted reserve forces.

Browning said that it was not ideology* that drove the killers. The 500 men in Battalion 101 did not have a Nazi affiliation. Indeed, it was entirely possible that their lives in the working-class, socialist city of Hamburg may have made them critical of the regime. Yet, although they were offered the opportunity to not to kill Jewish civilians, when told to shoot, around 80 percent of the policemen did so. Why?

To help him answer that question, Browning turned to the experiments of the American psychologist Stanley Milgram.* Milgram had found that people have a propensity to obey authority figures, even when those orders mean inflicting pain on others. Building on this, Browning argued that men became killers for reasons that seem mundane: fear of losing face, loyalty to comrades, anxiety about job promotion, or lack of moral reflection. The Holocaust was not caused by a unique form of German prejudice against Jews, of anti-Semitism.* It was brought about by human flaws present in much of the bureaucratic and modern West. Browning uncovered the mindset of a group of mass murderers—and revealed "ordinary men."

Why Does *Ordinary Men* Matter?

One sign of a book's importance is its ability to cause debate, and *Ordinary Men* is no exception. Browning's case study was of huge interest to sociologists and social psychologists who wanted to understand why genocide*—the systematic and deliberate destruction of a racial or ethnic group—happens. The work was almost universally praised by historians. One notable exception, however, was the response of American author Daniel Jonah Goldhagen.* Goldhagen was incensed by Browning's description of Reserve Police Battalion 101 as "ordinary." As a result he conducted his own research into both them and their motives, basing his findings on the same documents used by Browning. Goldhagen argued that these policemen were far from ordinary. Instead, he believed they had been consumed with a ferocious and centuries-old hatred of the Jews. Goldhagen went on to argue that this vicious anti-Semitism had been common to almost all Germans under the Nazis. This clash between Browning and Goldhagen is particularly interesting for students of history. It shows how two scholars can use the same sources but reach entirely different conclusions.

Ordinary Men is a crucial introduction to some of the most innovative scholarship on the Holocaust today. Browning's work explored the way violence escalated on the Eastern Front* during World War II, an area of study that is still being researched. However, scholars have moved on from Browning's preoccupation with the German psychology. The trend has moved away from trying to locate the roots of the Holocaust in German history or in the German national psyche. With the academic focus is now on the issue of wider instability and bloodshed in Eastern Europe. Seeing this type of killing in a broader political context means it might be more sensible to talk of multiple holocausts, rather than one single event.

Despite this, *Ordinary Men* remains an irreplaceable work. It was the first book that allowed a reader to see the Holocaust through the eyes of its perpetrators. It challenged readers to think about the human capacity to commit evil acts. And as well as having value as a documentary record, *Ordinary Men* offers a valuable moral from history. Browning's book warns that only a slender line prevents "ordinary men" from doing extraordinary—and terrible—things.

SECTION 1
INFLUENCES

THE AUTHOR AND THE HISTORICAL CONTEXT

KEY POINTS

- *Ordinary Men* remains a classic study of human motivation and how ordinary people can do extraordinary things.

- Browning wanted to understand how certain social systems could lead to ordinary men becoming complicit in crimes.

- Browning was profoundly influenced by the war crimes reported in Vietnam* and the corruption of the Watergate* scandal.

Why Read This Text?

Ordinary Men: Reserve Police Battalion 101 and the Final Solution in Poland is a surprising title for a work about a group of Nazi* policemen who were responsible for the deaths of 80,000 Jews* during World War II.* Christopher Browning's task is to prove to us that his title is appropriate. His book focuses on one case study: Reserve Police Battalion 101,* a group of policemen from Hamburg, in northern Germany. After Germany invaded Poland in 1939 the men of Battalion 101 oversaw the deportation of thousands of Jews from Poland to extermination camps. As the war progressed they also obeyed orders to shoot thousands of unarmed men, women, and children at point-blank range. Browning argued that these policemen were not monsters, distorted into vicious beasts by anti-Semitism.* Instead they were ordinary men, motivated by peer pressure and a sense of the national emergency affecting their country. *Ordinary Men* is a classic study of human motivation, its aim being to show how ordinary people can be persuaded to do extraordinary and inhuman things.

> **"** From the Nazi 'war of destruction' in eastern Europe
> and the 'war against the Jews' to the 'war without
> mercy' in the Pacific and most recently Vietnam,
> soldiers have all too often tortured and slaughtered
> unarmed civilians and helpless prisoners and committed
> numerous atrocities ... War, and especially race
> war, leads to brutalization, which leads to atrocity.
> This common thread, it could be argued, runs from
> Bromberg and Babi Yar through New Guinea and
> Manila and on to My Lai. **"**
>
> Christopher Browning, *Ordinary Men*

Ordinary Men was a bestseller when it was published in 1992. It came out at the right time. Americans and Europeans were fascinated by the Holocaust* in the 1990s, as the end of the Cold War* and the reunification of Germany* brought the tragedy back into the public eye. And never before had the crimes and motivations of a particular group been studied in such painstaking detail. *Ordinary Men* raised important and unsettling questions about how these crimes had occurred and whether they could happen again.

Author's Life

Born in 1944, Browning grew up in Chicago as the son of a philosophy professor and a school nurse. It was an academic, liberal household, where Browning learned to adopt a tolerant, thoughtful attitude towards modern problems and this would come through in all his work, including *Ordinary Men*. He was also affected by the political events of his school years. In the 1950s and 1960s America was riven with conflict, especially during the time of the Civil Rights Movement* and protests against the war in Vietnam that America was involved in. Browning was struck by the incredible violence of the military campaign there, as well as the violation of public trust the infamous Watergate political scandal had led to—with its implication of top American political figures in underhand and illegal activities. Browning wanted to understand how and why "good" people could become implicated in terrible crimes.

When he initially became interested in these questions, Browning was in graduate school. At the time he was studying French history. But he came across two authors who convinced him that his questions could best be understood by studying the Holocaust. These were the Austrian-born American historian Raul Hilberg* and the German-born political theorist Hannah Arendt.* In the 1960s, although it seems hard for us to believe now, the Holocaust was not a popular or prestigious topic for historical research. Yet driven by his desire to understand human nature, Browning chose it anyway. He has gone on to become one of the most distinguished Holocaust historians of his generation.

His first book, 1978's *The Final Solution and the German Foreign Office*, looked at German bureaucrats and how they implemented the country's Jewish policy in the East. In this work Browning attempted to understand how government bureaucrats could plan and administer murderous policies from the comfort of their offices.[1] Following this, Browning then turned his attention to the "ordinary men" on the front line, those who were actually committing the crimes.

Author's Background

Christopher Browning matured as a scholar in tumultuous times. As the student radicals of the 1960s marched against the Vietnam War, America was splitting in two. Like many in academic homes, Browning had been raised as a liberal: opposed to the war, but unsympathetic to the wild-eyed radicals engaging in terrorist acts. Such as the Weather Underground,* a left-wing terrorist organization headquartered in Browning's home city of Chicago. By the time

Browning was in graduate school (in Madison, Wisconsin, another hotbed of radical activism) headlines were blaring the news of America's wartime atrocities. Appalling crimes were being committed in Vietnam (the most notorious of these being the 1968 My Lai Massacre,* in which American soldiers killed at least 350 unarmed civilians). Browning began to wonder how good men—the people he had grown up with—could become bad men and war criminals.[2] These questions would eventually feed into *Ordinary Men*.

Browning was in Germany in 1972, researching his dissertation, when the Watergate scandal broke. Individuals connected with the Republican* administration burgled the headquarters of the Democratic* Party and it later came out that Richard Nixon,* then Republican president of the United States, had abused his privileges in multiple ways. The scandal led to Nixon's resignation in 1974. As Browning said later, "The dynamics of the Foreign Office's involvement in Jewish policy were not so different from the Watergate team players."[3]

NOTES

1   Christopher R. Browning, *The Final Solution and the German Foreign Office: A Study of Referat D III of Abteilung Deutschland, 1940–1943* (New York: Holmes & Meier, 1978).

2   Adam Shatz, "Browning's Version: A Mild-Mannered Historian's Quest to Understand the Perpetrators of the Holocaust," *Lingua Franca* 7, no. 2 (1997): 51.

3   Shatz, "Browning's Version," 52.

ACADEMIC CONTEXT

KEY POINTS

- After 1960 a generation of historians began trying to understand how the Holocaust* could have occurred.

- In the 1970s and 1980s opinion was divided about whether the Holocaust happened because of the way the war unfolded (the functionalist* interpretation) or because Hitler* had always intended to eradicate the Jewish* people in Europe (the intentionalist* interpretation).

- Browning's position was influenced by the work of historians Raul Hilberg* and Hannah Arendt.*

The Work in its Context

By the time Christopher Browning published *Ordinary Men* the Holocaust was a well-established area of study, but it had been seriously neglected in the first decade or two after the end of World War II.* When the Austrian-born American historian Raul Hilberg began his research in this area in 1948 he was highly isolated and struggled to find a publisher. It was only in 1960 and the trial of the Nazi* war criminal Adolf Eichmann* that scholars began to take notice of the subject.[1] Academics had initially concentrated on the actions of the Nazi elite and the supposedly all-powerful will of their leader Adolf Hitler.* After Eichmann's trial they started to reconstruct the other groups caught up in the Holocaust. These included officers of the German army (the Wehrmacht*), professionals such as Nazi doctors, and the Jewish victims themselves.

Writing about the Holocaust remains one of the most daunting and delicate tasks for any historian. Scholars from all disciplines have

> ❝ Particularly for the German occupiers stationed in the conquered lands of eastern Europe—literally tens of thousands of men from all walks of life—the mass-murder policies of the regime were not aberrational or exceptional events that scarcely ruffled the surface of everyday life. As the story of Reserve Police Battalion 101 demonstrates, mass murder and routine had become one. Normality itself had become exceedingly abnormal. ❞
>
> Christopher Browning, *Ordinary Men*

agreed that the enormity of the suffering involved makes it an almost inexplicable, or unrepresentable, event.[2] In the 1980s, German scholarship was rocked by what is known as the *Historikerstreit,** or "historians' quarrel." This was a fierce row over whether Nazi atrocities could be compared to the killings carried out at the same time by the communist* regime in the Soviet Union.* There was also disagreement over how far historians should even try to see the war through the eyes of the Nazis.

These debates continue. Some fear that trying to understand the Holocaust objectively somehow diminishes its status as an event unlike any other.[3] Others fear using the Holocaust for political, commercial, or any other type of gain cheapens it. Many believe this subject imposes a major moral responsibility on the scholar. As the Canadian historian Michael Marrus* asks, "Can those who write history be trusted with the Holocaust?"[4]

Overview of the Field
Before the 1990s, historians of the Holocaust were roughly split into intentionalist and functionalist camps. Functionalists, like the prominent German historian Hans Mommsen,* argued that the

Holocaust was neither foreseen nor calculated. Instead, it was the result of a gradual and unplanned process of radicalization among the Nazi Party leadership over the course of the war.[5] Mass murder developed in response to opportunity. The conquest of huge swathes of territory in Eastern Europe brought the Nazis into contact with many more of their enemies. Mass murder was also encouraged by internal dynamics within the Nazi Party, as different leaders in different departments sought to go further than their rivals. For many functionalists, the decisive shift from persecution to extermination came with the Nazi invasion of the Soviet Union in 1941. The danger of communism—an enemy outside Germany's borders—intensified the fear of the Jews, as an enemy "within" Germany's borders.

In contrast, intentionalists argued that the Holocaust was a deliberate and premeditated plan by the Nazi hierarchy.[6] They emphasized the personality of the German leader Adolf Hitler, highlighting the vitriolic hatred, especially of Jews, expressed in his speeches and in his best-selling memoir *Mein Kampf*.[7] Due to the cult of personality—the encouraged adoration of a living national leader—surrounding Hitler, he was able to impose his views on his followers. Intentionalists highlight that the campaign against the Jews began early in the Third Reich,* when the Nazis came to power. A boycott of Jewish shops and the burning of books by Jewish authors was already happening in the spring of 1933. Intentionalists believe that Hitler intended to destroy the Jewish presence in Germany and he took every opportunity to realize this goal.

Academic Influences

The work Browning produced in *Ordinary Men* was influenced by two major figures, the Austrian-born American historian Raul Hilberg and the German-born political theorist Hannah Arendt. Indeed, *Ordinary Men* is even dedicated to Hilberg. Hilberg is seldom read today, but he was a pioneering historian of the Holocaust and one of the first people to bring Holocaust historiography (or the study of the Holocaust) out of the world of polemical discourse* and into that of proper historical method. Browning read Hilberg while in the hospital recovering from an illness and he later described the encounter in religious terms, calling it a "conversion" experience.[8] Hilberg's key idea was that the historian could not understand the Holocaust as a massive, singular phenomenon: it was too large for that. Instead, it needed to be broken down and understood as countless personal and bureaucratic actions. "It may be possible," Hilberg wrote, "to view the entire design [of the Holocaust] as a mosaic of small pieces, each commonplace and lusterless by itself. Yet this progression of everyday activities, these notes, memoranda, and telegrams, embedded in habit, routine, and tradition, were fashioned into a massive destruction process."[9]

Hannah Arendt was also a major influence on Browning's work. Her controversial book *Eichmann in Jerusalem* (1963) made many Americans interested in the Holocaust and the problem of evil. In a bid to understand the psychology of the Nazis, Arendt attended the trial of Adolf Eichmann,* one of the worst of the Nazis. Her conclusion was that Eichmann was not a remarkable individual at all. He was merely a dim bureaucrat who was following orders and trying to move up in the organization. Describing this, Arendt used the term "the banality of evil." Browning did not call the massacres committed by Reserve Police Battalion 101 "banal." However, he was clearly influenced by Arendt's belief that the Holocaust cannot be explained simply by saying its perpetrators were evil.

NOTES

1   Michael Marrus, *The Holocaust in History* (Toronto: Key Porter Books, 2000), 201.

2   Saul Friedländer, *Probing the Limits of Representation: Nazism and the Final Solution* (Cambridge, MA: Harvard University Press, 1992).

3   Marrus, *The Holocaust in History*, 201–2.

4   Marrus, *The Holocaust in History*, 202.

5   See Hans Mommsen, "Cumulative Radicalisation and Progressive Self-Destruction as Structural Determinants of the Nazi Dictatorship," in *Stalinism and Nazism: Dictatorships in Comparison*, eds. Ian Kershaw and Moshe Lewin (Cambridge: Cambridge University Press, 1997), 75–87.

6   For important examples of the intentionalist position, see Yehuda Bauer, *A History of the Holocaust* (New York: F. Watts, 1982); Eberhard Jäckel and Jürgen Rohwer, eds., *Der Mord an den Judem im Zweiten Weltkrieg: Entschlußbildung und Verwirklichung* (Stuttgart: Deutsche Verlag-Anstalt, 1985).

7   Adolf Hitler, *Mein Kampf*, 2 vols. (Munich: Franz Eher Nachfolger, 1925–6).

8   Adam Shatz, "Browning's Version: A Mild-Mannered Historian's Quest to Understand the Perpetrators of the Holocaust," *Lingua Franca* 7, no. 2 (1997): 51.

9   Raul Hilberg, *The Destruction of the European Jews*, 3rd ed. (New Haven, CT: Yale University Press, 2003), 3:1060.

MODULE 3
THE PROBLEM

KEY POINTS

- The major question at the time Browning was writing was: why did German citizens actively take part in murder in accordance with the policies of the Nazi* regime?

- Browning was influenced by the findings of the American social psychologist Stanley Milgram.* Milgram's experiments suggested that most people will obey orders given by an authority figure.

- Browning approached the Holocaust* as a social historian,* crafting a microhistory* of a single battalion.

Core Question

Shocked by the scale of the devastation, historians asked how the human tragedy of the Holocaust could happen. The answers they were looking for were not simply practical. How far was it planned? When was the order to exterminate the Jews* given? They were also ethical. Why did thousands of individuals who had previously been law-abiding and even morally upstanding go on to commit cruel and murderous acts? This was a question that had real resonance when Christopher Browning was conducting his archival research for *Ordinary Men*. At the time the news headlines in his native America were all about American atrocities in the Vietnam War* and the political scandal of Watergate.* By studying the greatest crime of the twentieth century, the Holocaust, Browning wanted to gain a deeper insight into the overall human condition and mankind's capacity for evil.

> ❝ The policemen in the battalion who carried out
> the massacres and deportations, like the much smaller
> numbers who refused or evaded, were human beings. I
> must recognize that in the same situation, I could have
> been either a killer or an evader—both were human—if
> I want to understand and explain the behavior of both
> as best I can. This recognition does indeed mean an
> attempt to empathize. What I do not accept, however,
> are the old clichés that to explain is to excuse, to
> understand is to forgive. Explaining is not excusing,
> understanding is not forgiving. ❞
>
> Christopher Browning, *Ordinary Men*

The title of Browning's book *Ordinary Men* says a lot. The men of
Reserve Police Battalion 101* certainly were "ordinary" in a sense.
They were not fanatical Nazis, hardened by years spent fighting
Russians at the front in World War II.* They were middle-aged
policemen who had avoided the horrors of war to a large degree. Yet,
after some initial reluctance, these men were participants in terrible
massacres. During 1941 and 1942 they turned into hardened killers,
responsible for the deaths of around 80,000 Jews: men, women, and
children.

The Participants

Browning's work appeared at a time when there was great debate over
how to study the Holocaust. Intentionalists* believed that Hitler* had
always planned to massacre Europe's Jews and had waited for the
opportunity to put his plan into action. Functionalists* said that the
Holocaust was not Hitler's master plan, but arose in a chaotic way out
of events on the battlefield and from bureaucrats looking to make a
name for themselves back in Berlin.

Understanding why the Holocaust had happened was related to the issue of why so many Germans had been willing to carry it out. Some scholars chose to focus on perceived oddities of the German national character. One influential idea was the *Sonderweg** thesis. Meaning "special path," this was the argument that Germany had somehow developed in a special way, making the country different from other European nations, with a political system that was particularly authoritarian and not at all liberal. Many sociologists, however, resisted this narrowly German explanation of the Holocaust. They tried to highlight the growth of bureaucracy in many modern states. This bureaucracy created systems that valued obedience, efficiency, and logistical problem-solving above moral judgement.[1]

Bureaucratic growth partly explained why clerks had processed the paperwork of the Holocaust from afar. But what about the men who inflicted the actual violence face to face? In attempting to explain this, Browning became interested in the findings of the American social psychologist Stanley Milgram. In the early 1960s Milgram had carried out a famous experiment. It demonstrated that many individuals would willingly commit acts of terrible violence if instructed to do so by men of authority. Milgram also speculated about the importance of peer pressure in shaping individual behavior. These conclusions—if correct—meant that going along with immoral orders was not an issue that was unique to Germany.

The Contemporary Debate

Browning did not explicitly call himself either a functionalist or an intentionalist. However, his book pays little attention to Nazi leader Adolf Hitler or to the Nazi movement in general. This signals Browning's natural leaning towards the functionalist view of the Holocaust: the belief that violence on the ground in Eastern Europe arose as a result of geopolitical, economic, and military events.

As Browning points out in his book, however, the functionalists could not explain how and why the actual soldiers on the ground had carried out their crimes. Drawing on the work of Stanley Milgram, Browning argues that the soldiers were motivated by psychological factors such as obedience and peer pressure. In this way, he tries to provide a history of the Holocaust that maintains the functionalist emphasis on bureaucratic structures, but also retains the moral seriousness of the intentionalists and their emphasis on individual responsibility.

Browning's work also responds to the rise of "social history." Since the mid-1970s, history departments in America had become increasingly interested in recovering the voices of "ordinary men and women," those who lived and worked outside the halls of power. One of the most remarkable features of *Ordinary Men* is the close attention Browning pays to unremarkable and comparatively unimportant individuals, using their very normality as the key to unlocking broader historical processes. Reconstructing the actions of Reserve Police Battalion 101 allowed Browning to look at the "micro-history of a single battalion."[2]

NOTES

1   Zygmunt Bauman, *Modernity and the Holocaust* (Cambridge: Polity, 1989).

2   Christopher R. Browning, *Ordinary Men: Reserve Police Battalion 101 and the Final Solution in Poland* (London: Penguin, 2001), XVII.

MODULE 4
THE AUTHOR'S CONTRIBUTION

KEY POINTS

- Browning used the technique of microhistory* to demonstrate the very human qualities of the men who became killers in the police battalion.

- Browning did not believe that Germans were more evil than anyone else, rather that all people are capable of terrible acts in certain circumstances.

- Browning modified social psychologist Stanley Milgram's* findings to highlight the role of peer pressure as a motivation to action.

Author's Aims

It is important to understand precisely what Christopher Browning was trying to achieve in *Ordinary Men*. He was not trying to "explain" the Holocaust,* rather he was looking to understand how a group of middle-aged men, not at all notable for their Nazi* zeal, could commit terrible crimes.

The method he uses is the case study, or "microhistory." Unlike other Holocaust scholars, Browning does not study the broad sweep of economic, military, and racial policy. Instead, he focuses on Reserve Police Battalion 101,* a group responsible for some of the Holocaust's worst crimes. These were not the Nazi guards who ran the death camps* as mechanical factories of murder. This battalion often hunted down their victims in their homes and carried out murder in cold blood. These men were charged with shooting and burying thousands of Jews* in Poland. The Central Agency for the State Administration of Justice was the German office in charge of investigating Nazi

> 66 At the same time, however, the collective behavior of Reserve Police Battalion 101 has deeply disturbing implications ... Everywhere society conditions people to respect and defer to authority. Everywhere people seek career advancement. In every modern society, the complexity of life and resulting bureaucratization and specialization attenuate the sense of personal responsibility of those implementing official policy. Within virtually every social collective, the peer group exerts tremendous pressures on behavior and sets moral norms. If the men of Reserve Police Battalion 101 could become killers under such circumstances, what group of men cannot? 99

Christopher Browning, *Ordinary Men*

crimes following the foundation of the West German state in 1949. It was here that Browning uncovered details of the interrogations of the men from the battalion. He recalled, "Never before had I seen the monstrous deeds of the Holocaust so starkly juxtaposed with the human faces of the killers."[1] Browning wanted to understand how those ordinary people could have done what they did.

Approach

When *Ordinary Men* was published in 1992 it offered a unique contribution to a bitter debate about the nature and causes of the Holocaust. While there was an intellectual ancestry for his ideas, Browning brought fresh insight and fresh approaches to the topic. He was neither European nor Jewish, and his reasons for studying the Holocaust were different from those of most of the historians the subject has attracted. Browning was not interested in condemning Germany as an inherently violent nation. Neither was he trying, as other historians had, to condemn modernity itself as aggressively genocidal.*[2] Browning wanted to understand human nature itself and its ability to do evil. This is a question that has intrigued philosophers and theologians for thousands of years.

Browning claims that any human, in particular circumstances, can be goaded into committing acts of terrible violence. In arguing this, he drew on the work of the American social psychologist Stanley Milgram. Milgram had shown that ordinary individuals would inflict terrible pain on innocent test subjects if they were told to do so by an authority figure. Browning saw this all over the world, and throughout history. In his own lifetime, during the Vietnam War,* American soldiers had sent home pictures of themselves smiling and holding the skulls of their victims.[3] The problem of evil, Browning believed, was not a German problem, but a human one.

Contribution in Context

Browning himself said that his career "emerged very much amid the conflict between the approach to the Holocaust as a bureaucratic-administrative process on the one hand, and the view of the Holocaust as an ideological* crusade, on the other."[4] This administrative outlook was called the functionalist* position. The ideological position was called intentionalist.* Browning shared many of the functionalists' ideas. Yet in an important publication in 1981, Browning urged a leading functionalist, the German historian Martin Broszat,* to moderate his position. This sense of balance came to dominate Browning's work. His belief that the writing of history required proof kept him from adopting either the ideas of pure intentionalism or of pure functionalism. *Ordinary Men* is functionalist in that it pays very little attention to Nazi leader Adolf Hitler* or to the policy-making apparatus in Berlin. By studying the actions and personalities of a small group of people, Browning shows that personal intention and moral decisions mattered on the ground.

Browning also moved away from the notion that there was anything uniquely dysfunctional about German society. Instead he cited Stanley Milgram's experiments to show that many American citizens would also consent to inflicting pain when ordered to do so by authority figures. Yet Browning's findings did not tally entirely with Milgram's. Browning found that soldiers were more likely to be motivated by ties to their fellow soldiers than to their superiors.[5] If anything, this makes Browning's findings even more disturbing than Milgram's. While the link between authoritarianism and violence seems simple enough, Browning pointed out that our love for our comrades—the bonds that unite us with our classmates, teammates, or countrymen—may be just as dangerous.

NOTES

1 Christopher R. Browning, *Ordinary Men: Reserve Police Battalion 101 and the Final Solution in Poland* (London: Penguin, 2001), xiv.

2 Zygmunt Bauman, *Modernity and the Holocaust* (Cambridge: Polity, 1989).

3 Browning, *Ordinary Men*, 160.

4 Adam Shatz, "Browning's Version: A Mild-Mannered Historian's Quest to Understand the Perpetrators of the Holocaust," *Lingua Franca* 7, no. 2 (1997): 53.

5 Browning, *Ordinary Men*, 174–5.

SECTION 2
IDEAS

MAIN IDEAS

KEY POINTS

- *Ordinary Men* investigates three main themes: why men do evil things; the importance of internal group dynamics; and how violence is rationalized in hindsight.

- Browning showed how men who were not obvious Nazi* candidates became killers.

- The life of the police battalion was reconstructed with novelistic precision, creating intimate character portraits.

Key Themes

Christopher Browning's 1992 work *Ordinary Men* explored three major themes. The first examines how a group of "ordinary men" were gradually "initiated" into a campaign of continuous murder. Why did they comply with the order to kill? What do their actions tell us about the human propensity for evil? Browning avoided generalizations, saying: "The behavior of any human being is … a very complex phenomenon, and the historian who attempts to 'explain' it is indulging in a certain arrogance."[1] Nonetheless he believed that his research did shed light on what had happened.

Browning's second theme was the importance of group dynamics. Rather than succumbing to Nazi propaganda or anti-Semitic* hatred, Browning believed the men's bonds with one another were the crucial factor that led them to kill. In 1942, before the battalion carried out their first massacre, the men were all given the chance to opt out of the killing. Very few did. They did not want to appear to be cowards or to "lose face."[2] As the murder campaign continued, these bonds of solidarity tightened. The Nazi command deliberately encouraged

> **❝** But how did these men first become mass murderers? What happened in the unit when they first killed? What choices, if any, did they have, and how did they respond? What happened as the killing stretched on week after week, month after month? **❞**
>
> Christopher Browning, *Ordinary Men*

drunken celebrations on the day of what were called "actions." This helped some men blot out what had occurred. It let others think about the violence as sport.[3] This happened with what was known as the Jew Hunt of winter 1942, when German "hunters" tracked runaway Jews* like "prey" through the forests.[4]

Browning's third theme was how these men dealt with their crimes in hindsight. Between 1962 and 1972, 210 men from the battalion were interrogated as part of investigations carried out by the State Prosecutor in Hamburg. Browning speaks of the "candor and frankness" of their testimonies.[5] He highlights what these men omitted or suppressed from their accounts and how they rationalized and justified their conduct. Some argued that the 1940s were a radically different time and place, "as if they had been on another political planet."[6] Browning also notes their hypocrisy as they angrily accused Poles of betraying the Jews to the Nazis.[7] His book shows them recalling their pasts and wrestling uncomfortably with unforgivable deeds.

Exploring the Ideas

The American historian Daniel Jonah Goldhagen* saw the Nazi policemen as moral monsters, distorted by years of anti-Semitic propaganda. Browning saw Reserve Police Battalion 101* as a group of ordinary men faced with difficult moral questions in a time of war. He carefully reconstructs the lives and decisions of these middle-aged, working-class policemen from Hamburg, a city with a socialist past. Their age, class, and hometown all suggested they might be skeptical of the Nazi movement and there is little evidence that they bought into Hitler's anti-Semitic ravings and yet they committed terrible murders.[8] Browning shows the agony this caused, writing of officers who flung themselves to the ground in tears at what they had done.[9]

He also shows that around 80 percent of the policemen willingly took part in the massacres, even though those who opted not to were not punished. So why didn't more men avoid the killing? They had not been brutalized by war. They were not on the front lines and they had never seen combat.[10] Nor were they deeply anti-Semitic. Reflecting on the first massacre they carried out, in the Polish town of Jósefów* in July 1942, the policemen made scant mention of any anti-Semitic prejudices that motivated their actions. Browning describes the subject as a "glaring omission" in their testimony, "marked by silence."[11]

Instead, Browning argues that these men were driven by ordinary concerns: they were worried about the future of their nation, they wanted to win the war, and they wanted to support one another. Abstaining from the killing forced others to do more of the horrendous work and the military code of these policemen meant they were unwilling to do that. Finally, they did become brutalized through experience. Browning shows how difficult the men found the first massacre but within 15 months they had become seasoned killers. By October 1943, "long inured to the mass killing," their main discomfort was the smell caused by the bodies.[12] Browning's work tries to show how this process of desensitization occurred.

Language and Expression

Ordinary Men is meticulously researched. Browning tries to bring the flawed individuals of Reserve Police Battalion 101 to life. He draws unforgettable portraits of men like Major Wilhelm Trapp,* the commander of the battalion. Browning saw Trapp as a fundamentally decent man who found himself in a situation he could neither understand nor control. He did what he could to spare his men from the killing, allowing them not to participate if they so wished.[13] He clearly hated his orders and was seen weeping by many of his men.[14] But he still gave commands to kill. In September 1942, aware of the need to reach a set-target of deaths, Trapp ordered that 180 Jews and 78 Polish "accomplices" be taken out from the Kock ghetto* and shot. "Apparently the man who had wept through the massacre at Jósefów and still shied from the indiscriminate slaughter of Poles no longer had any inhibitions about shooting more than enough Jews to meet his quota."[15]

This is just one of many portraits that Browning provides. They allow us a better understanding of the Holocaust as a moral problem. However, Browning also advises caution and continuously highlights the difficulty of reconstructing exactly what had driven these policemen to act as they did. His work relies heavily on statements given in the 1960s, two decades after the war. "Each of these men played a different role. He saw and did different things. Each subsequently repressed or forgot certain aspects of the battalion's experiences, or reshaped his memory of them in a different way."[16] Browning refuses to leap to simple conclusions about their actions.

NOTES

1   Christopher R. Browning, *Ordinary Men: Reserve Police Battalion 101 and the Final Solution in Poland* (London: Penguin, 2001), 188.

2   Browning, *Ordinary Men*, 72.

3   Browning, *Ordinary Men*, 14.

4   Browning, *Ordinary Men*, 132.

5   Browning, *Ordinary Men*, xv.

6   Browning, *Ordinary Men*, 72.

7   Browning, *Ordinary Men*, 158.

8   Browning, *Ordinary Men*, 48.

9   Browning, *Ordinary Men*, 58.

10 Browning, *Ordinary Men*, 1.

11 Browning, *Ordinary Men,* 73.

12 Browning, *Ordinary Men*, 141.

13 Browning, *Ordinary Men*, 113, 130.

14 Browning, *Ordinary Men*, 58.

15 Browning, *Ordinary Men*, 102.

16 Browning, *Ordinary Men*, xvi.

MODULE 6
SECONDARY IDEAS

KEY POINTS

- Browning broadened public understanding of the horror of the Holocaust* by highlighting the millions of Jews* killed "face to face" rather than in the camps.

- Browning showed how the killing affected those who carried it out. It was so demoralizing that it was eventually franchised out to non-German units.

- One innovative but overlooked aspect of Browning's work was his interest in the comparative study of political violence.

Other Ideas

Christopher Browning's *Ordinary Men* helped the American public to understand the true character of the Holocaust as a historical phenomenon. The image most associated with the Holocaust is, of course, the concentration camp* (or the related extermination camp). Thanks to a large number of survivors' memoirs and testimonies, it is commonly assumed that most victims of the Holocaust were killed by poison gas, as in the notorious death chambers at Auschwitz-Birkenau.* This, however, is an inaccurate picture, as Browning's work helped to show. For one thing, much of the killing did not take place in the camps, but close to the victims' homes. Millions of Holocaust deaths were caused by gunshot. In blood-curdling detail, Browning shows us how these massacres worked. These were not the grimly efficient gassings of Auschwitz, but rather messy murders undertaken by drunken soldiers, often horrified at their own actions.

The men that Browning studied were part of the *Ordnungspolizei**

> ❝ These men were not desk murderers who could take refuge in distance, routine and bureaucratic euphemism that veiled the reality of mass murder. These men saw their victims face to face. ❞
>
> Christopher Browning, *Ordinary Men*

(or "Order Police"). They were originally supposed to supervise other police units in occupied Poland. However, as the Final Solution* to what was called the "Jewish Problem" became a reality in 1941 and 1942, they were drafted into the business of killing. The *Ordnungspolizei* were responsible for some of the exportation of people—guarding the trains that took Jews to the notorious camps. They were also charged with rounding up Jews and killing them. As Browning explains, "The personnel of the death camps was quite minimal. But the manpower needed to clear the smaller ghettos*—to round up and either deport or shoot the bulk of Polish Jewry—was not."[1]

Exploring the Ideas

In the summer of 1941, as the Soviet armies crumbled before the advance of the German forces into Russia, Adolf Hitler* and his henchman Heinrich Himmler* considered how to eliminate all the Jews in Europe. This couldn't be done by firing squad. A new method was needed, "one that was more efficient, less public, and less burdensome psychologically for the killers."[2] So the extermination camp network was constructed at Auschwitz-Birkenau, Chelmno,* Belzec,* and Sobibor.* But rounding up Jews, forcing them into ghettos and transporting them to the camps required a huge amount of manpower. This was where the *Ordnungspolizei* became indispensable, backed up by the assistance of *Trawnikis*,* units of volunteers from conquered territories in Ukraine, Lithuania, and

Latvia.[3] Browning's book looks at these "special actions" undertaken by the police throughout the Polish countryside in 1942. In doing so it shifts attention away from the mechanical process of the camps.

Yet Browning's account also reveals the profound demoralization the killing had on these policemen. This was not caused by their ethical or political principles. Few recognized the humanity of their Jewish victims. The nausea was caused by "the sheer horror of the killing process itself."[4] This demoralization became so pronounced that two new policies were introduced to counter it. First, on the spot massacres, like the one at Józefów,* were scaled back, with the bulk of the killing delegated to the extermination camp at Treblinka.* Second, the ugliest part of the round-up and ghetto clearances was carried out by units of *Trawnikis*. These concessions enabled the men of Reserve Police Battalion 101 to become "accustomed to their participation in the Final Solution," eventually emerging as "increasingly efficient and calloused executioners."[5]

Overlooked

One aspect of *Ordinary Men* that has not been emphasized is Browning's comparative approach. Today, global and comparative history* is universally valued. This was not the case when Browning was writing. Yet he still took the risk of comparing his own findings with what had happened in Japan and Vietnam. In particular, Browning cited the work of American historian John Dower* who had studied American military atrocities during the war in the Pacific* between 1941 and 1945.[6] In doing so, Browning undercut the conventional notion that the Holocaust was a unique, and uniquely German, phenomenon. He was suggesting that Americans, too, were also capable of committing similar crimes, even if they were on a much smaller scale.

This approach has not been picked up on by scholars, probably because Browning used it as evidence for the potential evil inherent in human nature. This is the least popular part of Browning's book, because it is a philosophical rather than an historical argument. For historians to incorporate the "comparative violence" aspect of Browning's work they would need to theorize about the different reasons why violence—and especially racial violence—happens so frequently in modern, mechanized wars.[7] That said, in recent years a comparative approach has begun to be more broadly applied to the subject of political violence. The label of genocide*—even Holocaust—has been applied controversially to a number of other instances of repression and violence. These include the violence used by General Francisco Franco* against his opponents in 1940s Spain once he had taken power after the civil war ended in 1939.[8]

NOTES

1   Christopher R. Browning, *Ordinary Men: Reserve Police Battalion 101 and the Final Solution in Poland* (London: Penguin, 2001), xiv.

2   Browning, *Ordinary Men*, 49.

3   Browning, *Ordinary Men*, 52.

4   Browning, *Ordinary Men*, 76.

5   Browning *Ordinary Men*, 77.

6   John Dower, *War Without Mercy: Race and Power in the Pacific War* (New York: Pantheon Books, 1986); Browning, *Ordinary Men*, 160.

7   For a version of how this might be done, see Mark Mazower, "Violence and the State in the Twentieth Century," *American Historical Review* 107 (2002): 1147–67.

8   Paul Preston, *The Spanish Holocaust: Inquisition and Extermination in Twentieth-century Spain* (London: HarperCollins, 2012).

MODULE 7
ACHIEVEMENT

KEY POINTS

- Browning successfully showed how the study of one group in the Holocaust* could raise broader questions about moral responsibility.

- The book was elegantly written, and appealed to scholars in sociology and social psychology studying the perpetrators of war crimes.

- Browning relied too much on Stanley Milgram,* who has been greatly criticized, for his psychological theory.

Assessing the Argument

In *Ordinary Men* Christopher Browning focuses on one unit involved in the Final Solution* to exterminate Jews.* He wanted to show how doing this could illustrate wider philosophical questions about why individuals choose to comply with immoral commands. He succeeded in his aim. *Ordinary Men* is crafted with great care and control and allows the reader to track both the mounting toll of Jewish victims in Poland and the impact this relentless killing had on the minds and memories of the policemen executioners. Browning successfully shifted focus away from the Nazi* leaders and the extermination camps to uncover the role of reserve units. Their killing campaigns, going from village to village, were a critical part of the Holocaust. By identifying how very mundane instincts—desire for promotion, fear of stepping out of line, bonding with peers—could lead to mass violence, Browning argues that his findings had "deeply disturbing implications" for other countries, not just Nazi Germany.[1]

> 66 The interrogations of 210 men from Reserve Police Battalion 101 remain in the archives of the Office of the State Prosecutor in Hamburg. They constitute the prime, indeed indispensable, source for this study. It is to be hoped that the admirable efforts of the prosecution in preparing this case will serve history better than they have served justice. 99
>
> Christopher Browning, *Ordinary Men*

Browning is more of a historian than a social theorist, however, he directly seeks to disprove social theories. For instance, he argues convincingly that anti-Semitism* was not the major motivation for the battalion's actions.[2] However, he doesn't offer a clear theory to take its place. Instead, he explores multiple causes that contributed to the men's behavior, stressing that while most policemen conformed and killed, there was always room for dissent and alternative choices. "The story of ordinary men is not the story of all men ... For even among them some refused to kill and others stopped killing. Human responsibility is ultimately an individual matter."[3]

Achievement in Context

Christopher Browning is among the most respected historians of the Holocaust in the world today. His success came late in his career. When *Ordinary Men* was published, Browning was teaching at Pacific Lutheran University, which is not an especially distinguished institution. The success of *Ordinary Men* propelled him to a prestigious professorship at the University of North Carolina. He is now also closely involved with Yad Vashem,* the Holocaust Museum in Israel, as well as the Holocaust Museum in America.

Ordinary Men appeared at a time when the study of genocide* and crimes against humanity was expanding.[4] Browning's core question "Why do men become mass murderers?" appealed to scholars from across the disciplines. The book analyzed the perpetrators of the Holocaust, and this was a novel approach, one that has borne fruit in the work of later historians and social psychologists. Its influence can be found in the work of German sociologist Harald Welzer* who, like Browning, has attempted to understand how ordinary men became implicated in mass killing. We can also look to the work of James Waller,* an American psychologist interested in similar themes. Browning himself doubtless welcomes more scholars working in this area. Indeed, he wrote the preface to one of Waller's works on the topic of mass violence.[5]

Limitations

Browning has not had a big influence outside the field of history. He is primarily a detail-oriented, archival historian, rather than a psychological or sociological theorist. While the evidence he collected has been inspiring to many, his particular interpretation of it has not been. Browning was heavily influenced by Stanley Milgram, an American social psychologist who, in a series of famous studies, showed that men were capable of inflicting great pain on innocent people if instructed to do so by recognized figures of authority. Milgram's studies, however, have been faulted in recent years, both on ethical grounds and for reasons of experimental design. David Mandel,* a Canadian sociologist, has particularly criticized the application of Milgram's ideas to the Holocaust. He has pointed out that every survivor of the Holocaust knows that all the perpetrators were not "just following orders," but in many cases were gleefully and unnecessarily punishing and debasing their victims.[6]

In Milgram's experiment, authority figures asked people (the subjects of the experiment) to administer increasingly painful electric shocks to other people. Unknown to the subjects, the "shockees" were played by actors. But the experimental design was criticized. Milgram used a limited sample of subjects who were predominantly middle-class individuals from New Haven, Connecticut. Milgram was also accused of taking advantage of the prestige held by scientists from Yale University (these were the "authority figures" from whom the subjects believed they were taking orders). In other words, Milgram's subjects were not "ordinary men," any more than Browning's were. The doubts cast on Milgram's framework in recent years in turn cast doubt on Browning's approach.[7] Browning's failure to take advantage of the most cutting-edge research in other disciplines has limited his impact outside the field of history.

NOTES

1 Christopher R. Browning, *Ordinary Men: Reserve Police Battalion 101 and the Final Solution in Poland* (London: Penguin, 2001), 188.

2 Browning, *Ordinary Men*, 178–83.

3 Browning, Ordinary Men, 188.

4 See Manus Midlarsky, *The Killing Trap: Genocide in the Twentieth Century* (Cambridge: Cambridge University Press, 2005).

5 James Waller, *Becoming Evil: How Ordinary People Commit Genocide and Mass Killing* (New York: Oxford University Press, 2002).

6 David Mandel, "The Obedience Alibi: Milgram's Account of the Holocaust Reconsidered," *Analyse & Kritik* 20 (1998): 74–94.

7 The path-breaking critique here was Martin T. Orne and Charles H. Holland, "On the Ecological Validity of Laboratory Deceptions," *International Journal of Psychiatry* 6 (1968): 282–93. For a more recent version, see Stephen Reicher and S. Alexander Haslam, "Obedience: Revisiting Milgram's Shock Experiments," in *Social Psychology: Revisiting the Classic Studies*, eds. Joanne R. Smith and S. Alexander Aslam (London: Sage, 2012).

MODULE 8
PLACE IN THE AUTHOR'S WORK

KEY POINTS

- Browning's work has two main strands. It looks at the evolution of Nazi* policy, and how this policy may be understood through specific case studies.

- *Ordinary Men* was not Browning's first work, but it was the first that went beyond a functionalist* argument that the Holocaust* wasn't pre-planned to investigate the realities of how the murder of Jews* actually took place on the ground.

- *Ordinary Men* established Browning's reputation as a moral commentator on the Third Reich.*

Positioning

Ordinary Men is Christopher Browning's most popular book, but it is important to view it in the context of his overall body of work. His first publication, *The Final Solution and the German Foreign Office* (1978), grew out of his dissertation. It studies the same events as *Ordinary Men*, but from a very different perspective.[1] *Ordinary Men* focuses on individuals who actually carried out Holocaust crimes. *The Final Solution and the German Foreign Office* analyzes the bureaucrats who planned and administered the Final Solution* from afar.

Throughout his career, Browning allied himself with functionalist interpreters of the Holocaust. Rather than seeing the Holocaust as an ideological crusade, explained primarily by Nazi leader Adolf Hitler's* anti-Semitism,* Browning believed it was a massive military and bureaucratic phenomenon—a phenomenon planned by a network of administrators with their own interests and intentions. In

> 66 Within the context of the murderous 'war of destruction' against the Soviet Union, the leap from the disappearance of the Jews 'sometime, somehow' to 'mass murder now' was taken in the summer of 1941. Once underway on Soviet territory, this ultimate or Final Solution beckoned to the Nazi regime as a solution for the rest of Europe's Jews as well. Already in the midst of committing mass murder against millions of Jews and non-Jews on Soviet territory, 'ordinary' Germans would not shrink from implementing Hitler's Final Solution for the Jews of Europe as well. 99
>
> Christopher Browning, *The Origins of the Final Solution*

The Final Solution and the German Foreign Office he showed that the Final Solution was not an all-encompassing, inescapable plan, but a project that arose from the bickering of bureaucrats more interested in their own careers than in annihilating European Jewry.

This argument is picked up in *Ordinary Men*. Here, Browning reveals the extent to which policy was improvised on the ground. He suggests that commanders in Eastern Europe did not wait for directives from above, but "correctly intuited and anticipated the wishes of the Führer"* when it came to Jewish policy.[2]

Integration

This interpretation of the Holocaust is present in Browning's other works, notably *The Origins of the Final Solution* (2004).[3] Offering a wider perspective than *Ordinary Men*, this work was commissioned by Yad Vashem,* the Holocaust museum in Israel and the global center of Holocaust knowledge and consciousness. This book is less about the "why" than the "how" of the Holocaust. It maps the evolution of Nazi policy across the crucial years of the war. This approach allowed

Browning to restate his version of the functionalist thesis and to underline the transformative effect that the invasion of the Soviet Union* had on Nazi thinking. Before the 1941 invasion, the Nazis had considered a range of policies regarding the Jews. These included forced emigration, deportation, and segregation. Indeed, Browning describes Poland as the "laboratory of racial policy," an arena in which a host of different ideas could be tried out.[4] However, Browning argues that the decisive shift towards a policy of systematic extermination occurred between September and October 1941.[5]

This chronology has been contested, leading to a dispute between Browning and the German Holocaust historian Peter Longerich.* A quarrel over dates may seem minor, but it reveals Browning's desire to relate overall wartime policy to the activities of Reserve Police Battalion 101.* The esteemed American historian of Germany Geoff Eley* has praised both Longerich and Browning for getting beyond the "excessively Berlin-centered and administrative viewpoint" and moving "assuredly back and forth between the decision-makers in Berlin and the complexities of action in the field." Eley adds that while this synthesis is impressive, it has tended to leave out the viewpoint of the Jewish victims.[6] Browning has tried to correct this in some of his other publications. These include a collection of rediscovered letters written by one family of Polish Jews in Krakow between 1939 and 1942.[7] So Browning's overall work is divided between big works of interpretation—mapping the growth of Nazi policies—and "microhistories"* that explore how these policies affected both perpetrators and victims alike.

Significance

The importance of *Ordinary Men* was realized from the moment it was published in 1992. Writing in the prestigious *New York Times Books Review*, the American psychiatrist Walter Reich* hailed Browning's work on the perpetrators. It "helps us understand, better than we did before, not only what they did to make the Holocaust happen but how they were transformed psychologically from the ordinary men of his title into active participants in the most monstrous crime in human history."[8]

Ordinary Men was the foundation of Browning's authority as a commentator on the Holocaust. Following its publication he was asked to serve as an expert witness against those who denied the Holocaust. In 2000 Browning was a lead witness in the explosive libel case brought in London by the English author David Irving.* Irving was suing Penguin Books for having published a refutation of his scholarship. Browning was one of a handful of prominent historians who testified at the trial and his testimony was seen as decisive in proving the authenticity of the Holocaust once and for all.[9] Browning's reputation as someone who wanted to raise awareness of the Holocaust was further enhanced by his work with Yad Vashem.

In his later work Browning has continued to take a marked interest in how detailed studies of particular communities can deepen our understanding of World War II.* A good example of this can be seen in his book *Remembering Survival: Inside a Nazi Slave-Labor Camp* (2014). Browning found his material for this in the legal records of another failed prosecution of the 1970s. This had been brought against the German chief of Starachowice, a town in Poland. He had been responsible for liquidating the nearby ghetto,* sending thousands to extermination camps and condemning 1,600 other Jews to slave labor. Through the testimonies of 300 survivors, Browning was able to commemorate the suffering, resilience, and ingenuity of many ordinary Jewish families, again laying bare the moral dimension and human costs of the Holocaust.[10]

NOTES

1 Christopher R. Browning, *The Final Solution and the German Foreign Office: A Study of Referat D III of Abteilung Deutschland, 1940–1943* (New York: Holmes & Meier, 1978).

2 Christopher R. Browning, *Ordinary Men: Reserve Police Battalion 101 and the Final Solution in Poland* (London: Penguin, 2001), 12.

3 Christopher R. Browning, *The Origins of the Final Solution: The Evolution of Nazi Jewish Policy, September 1939–March 1942* (Lincoln, NE: University of Nebraska Press, 2004).

4 Browning, *Origins of the Final Solution*, 12.

5 Christopher R. Browning, *Nazi Policy, Jewish Workers, German Killers* (Cambridge: Cambridge University Press, 2000), 31, 55.

6 Geoff Eley, *Nazism as Fascism: Violence, Ideology and the Ground of Consent in Germany 1930–1945* (London and New York: Routledge, 2013), 176.

7 Christopher R. Browning, *Every Day Lasts a Year: A Jewish Family's Correspondence from Poland* (Cambridge: Cambridge University Press, 2007).

8 Walter Reich, "The Men who Pulled the Triggers," *New York Review of Books*, April 12, 1992.

9 D. D. Guttenplan, *The Holocaust on Trial* (New York: Norton, 2001), 210–14.

10 Christopher R. Browning, *Remembering Survival: Inside a Nazi Slave-Labor Camp* (New York: Norton, 2010).

SECTION 3
IMPACT

MODULE 9
THE FIRST RESPONSES

KEY POINTS

- The American author Daniel Jonah Goldhagen* suggested that the subjects of *Ordinary Men* were not ordinary at all, but were motivated by an irrational anti-Semitism* that dominated German society.

- Browning believed that Goldhagen exaggerated the extent of popular anti-Semitism before the war.

- Browning's high-profile, often fractious, debate with Goldhagen showed how two historians could draw different conclusions from the same body of evidence

Criticism

Critics of Christopher Browning's work *Ordinary Men* can be divided into two camps: the American author Daniel Jonah Goldhagen—and everyone else. In 1992 Goldhagen wrote a lengthy and highly critical review of *Ordinary Men*.[1] Then, in 1997, he published his own book, *Hitler's Willing Executioners*. Using the same evidence as Browning (the interrogation records of Reserve Police Battalion 101*) Goldhagen came to radically different conclusions.[2] The book caused a sensation. Goldhagen appeared on television and radio talk shows, and entire conferences were devoted to exploring his controversial ideas.

Goldhagen believed that the Holocaust* was caused, above all, by centuries of German anti-Semitism. In *Hitler's Willing Executioners* he argued that Germans in general were enthusiastic about committing mass murder. Taking a direct swipe at Browning's depiction of the Reserve Police Battalion 101, Goldhagen insisted that "the unreal images of them as isolated, frightened, thoughtless beings performing

> ❝ I disagree with essential features of Browning's
> portrait of the battalion, with many of his explanations
> and interpretations of particular events, even with some
> of his assertions of fact, and especially with his overall
> interpretation and explanation of the men's actions ...
> the frequent absence or misinterpretation of evidence
> that suggests the general voluntarism and approval of
> the men in the battalion for their genocidal activities ... ❞
>
> Daniel Jonah Goldhagen, *Hitler's Willing Executioners*

their tasks reluctantly are erroneous."[3] In his view, Browning had not read the courtroom statements critically. He was too willing to believe the men when they said they had not wanted to kill, or that many of them had chosen not to. Of course they down played their murderous anti-Semitism, Goldhagen argued, they were on trial for their lives.

Goldhagen made some good points, but he expressed them in a highly combative and unscholarly manner. The Israeli-born historian Omer Bartov,* however, offered a different critical perspective on Browning's work. His review of *Ordinary Men* assessed the book as "not wholly satisfactory," arguing that Browning had left major questions unanswered. In what way are these men "ordinary"? They are Nazi policemen during wartime. Could we expect policemen in New York City to act the same way? "Does he imply," Bartov asks, "that anyone could be made into a mass murderer, no matter his education, social background, political convictions, and so forth?"[4]

Responses

Browning has been keen to respond to criticisms, particularly those leveled against him by Goldhagen. The debate is helpful for historians, as it provides a fascinating case of two scholars arguing fundamentally different theories that are based on the same body of facts.

The two academics clashed in many different places over the years: most notably at a 1996 conference at the United States Memorial Holocaust Museum. Goldhagen began with his traditional criticisms of Browning—that he was too willing to downplay the enthusiasm and brutality of the killers, playing up their "ordinary" qualities at the expense of their extraordinary crimes. Browning responded and, to a remarkable degree, refused to back down from his claims. Instead, he produced more evidence for them, including a letter he had received after the publication of *Ordinary Men*: "Your book deeply affected me," the letter said, "because I personally experienced the German *Schutzpolizei* [police]."[5] In the letter many of the policemen were described as being very kind and not exhibiting the demonic anti-Semitism* that Goldhagen saw at work in the Nazi soldiers. Goldhagen is blind to this, Browning suggested, because he subscribes to a narrow interpretation of German history in which every event in Germany from 1870 to 1945 is explained with reference to all-powerful anti-Semitism.

Conflict and Consensus

Browning refused to compromise his basic claims. He declared that Goldhagen's book *Hitler's Willing Executioners* oversimplified the Holocaust and pandered to a public that said, "We don't want complex answers, we just want an answer. We want to understand the Holocaust as we did fifty years ago—German culture is evil, it created evil people, who committed evil deeds."[6] This comment goes to the heart of the differences between Goldhagen and Browning. Goldhagen was extreme in his rhetoric, aiming to come up with a single overarching theory that denounced German society. Browning, much more sober in tone and cautious in his use of evidence, revealed the interaction of multiple factors.[7]

In an afterword to the 2001 edition of *Ordinary Men* Browning refuted Goldhagen's notion of a continuous and deeply held popular anti-Semitism in Germany. He showed that even when the Nazis were imposing anti-Jewish measures in the 1930s, the bulk of the population responded as indifferent onlookers, not ferocious anti-Semites.[8] He dismissed Goldhagen's argument that the German world view had been static and already formed by 1933.[9] Instead, Browning emphasized that the destructive war on the Eastern Front* had radicalized its participants.

Lastly, Browning emphasized that the perpetrators of the Holocaust were not just Germans.[10] He pointed out the dishonest "double standard" Goldhagen had used in selecting his evidence, concealing the extent to which the men of Reserve Police Battalion 101 had also shown great cruelty to Polish victims, and had also been conflicted and sickened by the killing of Jews.[11] They had not taken sadistic relish in the violence, but had sunk into alcoholism and self-pity to cope with the task. "That these policemen were 'willing executioners' does not mean that they 'wanted to be genocidal executioners.' This, in my opinion, is an important distinction that Goldhagen consistently blurs."[12]

NOTES

1 Daniel Jonah Goldhagen, "The Evil of Banality," *The New Republic*, July 13 and 20, 1992, 49–52.

2 Daniel Jonah Goldhagen, *Hitler's Willing Executioners: Ordinary Germans and the Holocaust* (New York: Vintage, 1997).

3 Goldhagen, *Hitler's Willing Executioners*, 406.

4 Omer Bartov, *Murder in Our Midst: The Holocaust, Industrial Killing, and Representation* (New York: Oxford University Press, 1996), 92–3.

5 Daniel J. Goldhagen, Christopher R. Browning, and Leon Wieseltier, *The "Willing Executioners"/"Ordinary Men" Debate* (Washington, DC: United States Holocaust Research Institute, 1996), 16.

6 Christopher Browning, quoted in A. D. Moses, "Structure and Agency in the Holocaust: Daniel J. Goldhagen and His Critics," *History and Theory* 37, no. 2 (1998): 196.

7   Christopher R. Browning, *Ordinary Men: Reserve Police Battalion 101 and the Final Solution in Poland* (London: Penguin, 2001), xviii.

8   Browning, *Ordinary Men*, 200–1.

9   Browning, *Ordinary Men*, 202–3.

10 Browning, *Ordinary Men*, 209.

11 Browning, *Ordinary Men*, 212–4.

12 Browning, *Ordinary Men*, 216.

THE EVOLVING DEBATE

KEY POINTS

- Browning's thesis has been challenged for not taking into account the impact of relentless propaganda in poisoning German attitudes towards Jews.*

- The German historian Peter Longerich* believes that Browning's focus was too narrow. As well as studying the actions of those who carried out the Holocaust,* the actions of its victims should be explored too.

- Browning opened the debate about the way in which overarching Nazi* policies were executed on the ground. This has allowed historians like Peter Longerich to show the interaction between what was happening at the center of power and what was happening out in the field.

Uses and Problems

The debate on the Holocaust has moved on since the 1992 publication of Christopher Browning's *Ordinary Men*. Browning's conclusions about Reserve Police Battalion 101* and its activities are broadly accepted, but the work is no longer at the forefront of academic research. However, it remains a classic text thanks to its use of archive materials, its emotional power, and its accessibility.

In the last 20 years historians have again looked at the role ideology* played in creating the Holocaust. While it is no longer acceptable to suggest that ideology alone explains events, recent scholars have suggested that Browning may have been too quick to overlook it. Browning's subjects had lived in Nazi* Germany for many years. He did not think that their anti-Semitism* was a very important factor, but other scholars disagree. The American historian

> ❝ A recent trend in historical scholarship places the onus of guilt on ordinary Germans for the perpetration of Nazi crimes ... But the recent trend in historical scholarship threatens to underestimate and obscure the enormous culpability and capability of the leading organs of the Nazi terror, such as the Gestapo, and to overestimate the culpability of ordinary German citizens. It needs to be remembered that some Germans were far more guilty than others. ❞
>
> Eric Johnson, *The Nazi Terror: Gestapo, Jews and Ordinary Germans*

Peter Fritzsche* has shown that Germans were assaulted with enormous amounts of propaganda in the 1930s, to the extent that most accepted at least some of Hitler's National Socialist ideology.[1] The Israeli-born historian Alon Confino* has recently called for new study into the ideology that made the Holocaust "thinkable."[2]

This return to an interest in ideology suggests that the police troops studied by Browning may not have been as "ordinary" as Browning believed. Academics have shown that the *Ordungspolizei* ("Order Police") were subjected to a course of intense ideological training.[3] Other branches of the Nazi police forces have also been reinterpreted. The American historian Eric Johnson* has provided an account of the way "ordinary Germans" were affected by dealings with the Gestapo. Johnson found that, unlike the reservists discussed by Browning, the troopers in the Gestapo had a significant prehistory in police and paramilitary organizations. These police, in many ways, were professionals in violent repression.[4]

Schools of Thought

Between the 1960s and the 1990s, many historians accepted that the Holocaust was directed by so-called "desk killers" in Berlin. Browning prompted research into the perpetrators themselves, suggesting that the Holocaust can only be understood through local studies of individuals on the Eastern Front.* While there is still interest in the activities of Berlin bureaucrats, Browning's position has been entirely accepted by historians like the German academic Andrej Angrick,* who has studied genocide* in Latvia.[5]

Other academics are exploring issues that Browning did not address. *Ordinary Men* was based on German sources and archives alone. Although non-German figures such as Nazi volunteers in Poland do appear among the perpetrators in Browning's work, they are not discussed or explored.[6] Now that the Holocaust is no longer viewed as a crime perpetrated by Germans alone, Browning's analysis of one German police unit can no longer explain the tragedy as a whole.

Another scholar, the German historian Peter Longerich, has argued against trying to pin down the dating of the decision for extermination too precisely, since Nazi policy towards the Jews remained fluid, even into 1942. Longerich also emphasized that the perpetrators of the Holocaust should not be studied in isolation. They were responsive to the actions of their victims. The Jews' freedom to act was profoundly constrained, but they were in some cases able to slow down the policies of annihilation—by fleeing into hiding, or by bribing or negotiating with local Nazis. Longerich is more sympathetic to Browning than to Daniel Jonah Goldhagen's view that Germans' long-standing and deep-seated anti-Semitism were to blame for the Holocaust; but Longerich sees both scholars as rather too one-sided, "concentrating exclusively on perpetrators and their activities." In his view the next phase of scholarship should try to understand the "parameters" in which all the perpetrators were working—parameters that were fixed by Jewish action too.[7]

In Current Scholarship

In *Ordinary Men* Browning took the reader away from the halls of Berlin to the killing fields of the Eastern Front. He showed how the killings took place and who was directly responsible for them—in this case the "ordinary men" of Reserve Police Battalion 101. He showed, too, that the Holocaust was not perpetrated by vicious anti-Semites, but by frightened men, driven by alcohol, camaraderie, and the demands of wartime. These were new—and stunning— insights.

Historians have accepted Browning's call to pay attention to the interaction between the political center of the war (Germany) and the periphery (in Eastern Europe). It was at the periphery that the action was actually taking place. The Nazi officer Adolf Eichmann*—who was in charge of much of the organization of the Holocaust—was not bound to his desk. Nor were his staff. They were all closely involved with the ground operations that Browning discusses.[8] The work of the German historians Peter Longerich and Jürgen Matthäus* shows how Browning's perspective can be usefully integrated with more traditional studies of the Nazi leadership.[9] Before Browning, historians thought it sufficient to detail the anti-Semitism of Nazi leaders alone. After Browning it became necessary to show how this anti-Semitism was translated into violence on the Eastern Front. As an example, Longerich showed that genocidal violence followed in the wake of leading Nazi Heinrich Himmler's* tours through Eastern Europe. It is clear from the context of Browning's overall work that he also saw the Holocaust in this way: as a dynamic interplay between central policy making and action on the ground.

NOTES

1   Peter Fritzsche, *Germans into Nazis* (Cambridge, MA: Cambridge University Press, 1998).

2   Alon Confino, *A World Without Jews: The Nazi Imagination from Persecution to Genocide* (New Haven, CT and London: Yale University Press, 2014).

3   For a new perspective on the Order Police, see Edward Westermann, "Shaping the Police Soldier as an Instrument for Annihilation," in *The Impact of Nazism: New Perspectives on the Third Reich and Its Legacy*, eds. Alan E. Steinweis and Daniel E. Rogers (Lincoln, NE: University of Nebraska Press, 2003), 129–50.

4   Eric Johnson, *Nazi Terror: The Gestapo, Jews and Ordinary Germans* (New York: Basic Books, 2000), 49.

5   Andrej Angrick, *Besatzungspolitik und Massenmord: Die Einsatzgruppe D in der südlichen Sowjetunion 1941–1943* (Hamburg: Hamburger Edition, 2003).

6   Christopher R. Browning, *Ordinary Men: Reserve Police Battalion 101 and the Final Solution in Poland* (London: Penguin, 2001), 52.

7   Peter Longerich, *Holocaust: The Nazi Persecution and Murder of the Jews* (Oxford: Oxford University Press, 2010), 3, 7.

8   George C. Browder, "Perpetrator Character and Motivation: An Emerging Consensus," *Holocaust and Genocide Studies* 17, no. 3 (2003): 480–97.

9   Jürgen Matthäus, "Controlled Escalation: Himmler's Men in the Summer of 1941 and the Holocaust in the Occupied Soviet Territories," *Holocaust and Genocide Studies* 21, no. 2 (2007): 218–42; Peter Longerich, *Heinrich Himmler: Biographie* (Munich: Siedler, 2008).

MODULE 11
IMPACT AND INFLUENCE TODAY

KEY POINTS

- *Ordinary Men* has made Browning one of the leading Holocaust* historians in America.

- Browning's arguments have been challenged by those who want to include further examinations of geography and politics in understanding the origins of the Holocaust.

- Browning's work is still important because it helps readers understand what it was like to actually be there where the killing was taking place.

Position

Christopher Browning's book *Ordinary Men* remains one of the most widely assigned works in European history courses and Browning's ongoing work has won him a reputation as the most perceptive and analytically acute historian of the Holocaust writing today. In the world of academia Browning's approach has conclusively won the day against his major opponent, the American author Daniel Jonah Goldhagen,* who has since moved onto different topics.

But Browning's thesis about the violent capacities of ordinary men has been modified since *Ordinary Men* was published in 1992. Increasing attention has been paid to the diversity of those who perpetrated the Holocaust. The men of Reserve Police Battalion 101,* so incisively described by Browning, were only one link in a much larger chain. The importance of long-term processes of subtle indoctrination has been highlighted. In a telling biography, the German historian Ulrich Herbert* revealed the ideological* beliefs and bureaucratic machinations of the mid-level Nazi* police chief

> ❝ In Jedwabne ordinary Poles slaughtered the Jews, very much as ordinary Germans from the *Ordnungspolizei* Battalion no. 101 did in Jósefów, as documented in Christopher Browning's *Ordinary Men*. They were men of all ages and of different professions; entire families on occasion, fathers and sons acting in concert ... Not anonymous men in uniform, cogs in a war machine, agents carrying out orders, but their own neighbors, who chose to kill and were engaged in a bloody pogrom— willing executioners. ❞
>
> Jan Gross, *Neighbors: The Destruction of the Jewish Community in Jedwabne, Poland*

Werner Best.* Herbert rooted Best's actions in the German ideological and political struggle of the 1920s and 1930s.[1] This time frame suggests there is a need to think about when the process of radicalization began, in some instances long before World War II.* The distinguished British-born sociologist Michael Mann* has also cast doubt on Browning's overall approach. In an article from 2000, Mann analyzed the biographies of 1,500 perpetrators of the Holocaust, concluding that most of them were not at all "ordinary men," but had in fact been involved in anti-Semitic violence for decades.[2]

Interaction
The limitations of Browning's approach are apparent, which is why few scholars have adopted it. The trend now is towards larger studies of the Holocaust, taking full account of the military, political, and strategic pressures that Nazi leader Adolf Hitler* faced. These accounts do not undercut Browning's efforts—his archival work is still unsurpassed—but they do change the emphasis placed on his

research.

A classic instance of this wide-scale approach is the American historian Timothy Snyder's* book *Bloodlands: Europe between Hitler and Stalin*. In this prize-winning work, Snyder demonstrated that the vast majority of the killing in early twentieth-century Europe was located at the troubled eastern boundaries of the continent, in countries such as Poland, the Baltic States, Belarus, and especially Ukraine.[3] These were territories that had previously belonged to the Hapsburg, Ottoman, or Russian Empires—empires that had disintegrated in the final stages of World War I,* leaving many minorities vulnerable in their wake. By adopting a wide time scale and comparing Nazi and Soviet* slaughter in the same places, Snyder is able to show the crucial role of geography in determining ethnic violence.

Another useful approach, which was not employed by Browning, is the attempt to understand the Holocaust in the light of Europe's imperial past. Many scholars, notably the British historian Mark Mazower,* have suggested that Europe's long experience of empire and racial subjugation may have played a role in the events of the 1940s.[4] Again, this approach does not directly contradict Browning's, but it does return to the broader historical frame that Browning rejected in *Ordinary Men*.

The Continuing Debate

Holocaust scholarship has moved on from Browning's question of "Why do men become mass murderers?" The questions being asked now are: "How were ordinary Germans formed by their experiences in the 1920s and 1930s? And to what extent was the Holocaust perpetrated by non-German Europeans, coming from a tradition of their own?" In *Neighbors*, a book in some ways comparable to *Ordinary Men*, the Polish-born American historian Jan Gross* reconstructed the murder of a community of Jews* in the Polish town of Jedwabne. This murder was carried out by Polish neighbors of the Jews, men and women with whom they had lived for generations. Gross reveals how the invasion and occupation of the German forces allowed a host of bitter grievances to suddenly flare up and for old scores to be settled. Mixed in were jealousy, greed, opportunism, and fear.[5] Like Browning, Gross explored the ways in which the experience of war, even if it did not include direct military service, can brutalize ordinary men into committing unspeakable acts.

Case studies that reveal the lived experience of the Holocaust help us to understand the terrible events of the mid-twentieth century in a way that other books can't. Snyder's *Bloodlands*,[6] for example, does much to place the Holocaust in the context of the mass military violence, committed by many countries, which gripped Eastern Europe during the 1930s and 1940s. Snyder draws on archives and uses languages that Browning does not. Nonetheless, Snyder gives no sense of what it was like to be there and what kind of men actually committed the crimes. *Ordinary Men* still does this better than any other scholarly work on the topic meaning that, although the scholarship itself has moved on, Browning's work is still keenly read.

NOTES

1 Ulrich Herbert, *Best: Biographische Studien über Radikalismus, Weltanschauung, und Vernunft, 1903–89* (Bonn: J. H. W. Diet, 1996).

2 Michael Mann, "Were the Perpetrators of Genocide 'Ordinary Men' or 'Real Nazis'? Results from Fifteen Hundred Biographies," *Journal of Genocide Studies* 14 (2000), 331–66.

3 Timothy Snyder, *Bloodlands: Europe between Hitler and Stalin* (New York: Basic Books, 2010).

4 Mark Mazower, *Hitler's Empire: Nazi Rule in Occupied Europe* (London: Allen Lane, 2008).

5 Jan Gross, *Neighbors: The Destruction of the Jewish Community in Jedwabne, Poland* (Princeton, NJ: Princeton University Press, 2001).

6 Snyder, *Bloodlands*.

MODULE 12
WHERE NEXT?

KEY POINTS

- *Ordinary Men* will remain a classic. It will, however, be fitted into a wider study of mass murder on the Eastern Front.*

- New work into the psychology of the Third Reich* considers how German citizens lived with their crimes afterwards. This complements Browning's work.

- Browning is both a historian and a moralist: his text combines details of a very specific incident with an inquiry into the universal aspects of human nature.

Potential

Christopher Browning's *Ordinary Men* is still one of the touchstones of Holocaust* scholarship in the English-speaking world. Its approach is out of date in some ways, but Browning's meticulous archival research, combined with his vivid writing, ensure that the book will continue to be admired and taught. There is no other historical text that brings the Holocaust to life like *Ordinary Men*.

That said, the work has become less relevant for scholars. There are two reasons for this. The first is that Browning's approach is now commonplace. We have many studies of the "perpetrators" of the Holocaust and no serious scholar still holds the old intentionalist* view that the Holocaust should be viewed simply as Adolf Hitler's* long-term plan, or that German anti-Semitism* led directly to the Holocaust. Nearly everyone now accepts some version of Browning's modified functionalism,* that the systematic killing of Jews* developed out of a particular set of circumstances.

> ❝ Indeed, Trapp's distress was a secret to no one. At the marketplace one policeman remembered hearing Trapp say, 'Oh, God, why did I have to be given these orders,' as he put his hand on his heart ... He said something like, 'Man ... Such jobs don't suit me. But orders are orders' ... Concerning Jósefów, Trapp later confided to his driver, 'If this Jewish business is ever avenged on earth, then have mercy on us Germans'. ❞
>
> Christopher Browning, *Ordinary Men*

However, most historians also believe there is significantly more to the story than this. Scholars have focused on the decades of ideological* training that even the "ordinary men" of Reserve Police Battalion 101* experienced in Hitler's Germany.[1] Today, historians see "the Holocaust" as a series of smaller holocausts, each undertaken by different perpetrators, at different times and for different reasons. Timothy Snyder* has shown how the actions of the Germans need to be seen within the wider context of the "bloodlands" of Eastern Europe.[2] Browning was aware of this, but he did not integrate this into his narrative, mainly because the archives in the East were not open when he was conducting his research. Browning's findings also need to be balanced against new revisionist work on Polish atrocities against Jews after the war.[3]

Future Directions

Current research is enriching the psychological insights Browning offered of the policemen in *Ordinary Men*. Scholars studying the cultural history of the Final Solution* aim to understand why the German population did so little to prevent it. Recent studies have tried to understand the mix of consent and coercion that kept Germans loyal to the regime. This is vital in understanding morale on the home front during the war years.[4] Browning's work shifted interest from the study of elites to ordinary men. This raises deep questions about how the killers interpreted their gruesome actions and justified them as "normal" and "necessary." The British historian Dan Stone* has said the Holocaust should be imagined "as the outcome of a German narrative through which the perpetrators made sense of the world."[5]

Browning's book revealed that the interrogations by the Hamburg Prosecutors Office in the 1960s were a dead end. They achieved only a handful of convictions and many cases were dropped. This was not unusual in this period,[6] but this sense of a lack of justice being seen to be done makes the question of how far the Holocaust was subsequently denied, repressed, or hidden in German society even more significant. A key issue for contemporary research into historical memory is "How were perpetrators able to adjust to post-war society?"[7] Browning ends his story with the war, but it would be interesting to discover how the men of the battalion learned to live with their crimes in the years that followed. The American historian Eric Johnson* has explored how information about mass murder circulated in Nazi Germany and how it continued to inform the memory of participants and survivors decades later.[8]

Summary

Ordinary Men is, without a doubt, a landmark in Holocaust literature. It was the first work to show what it was like to be a perpetrator of the Final Solution. For decades, students had been able to understand and inhabit the experience of the Holocaust's victims through literature and historical works; Browning's achievement was to provoke understanding of, if not sympathy with, the experience of the perpetrators. His work is therefore a critical step in historical understanding. Reading it is as much an ethical journey as a historical one.

Browning does not look to forgive the men of Reserve Police Battalion 101. He shares a sense of moral outrage with his readers. But his work shows that outrage is not enough. Browning believed that it was vital to use intellect and scholarly understanding to work through this feeling. The historian can then attempt to reconstruct the psychological and military context of the racial violence on the Eastern Front.

Paradoxically, Browning's achievement was both to localize and to universalize the Holocaust. He shows—in painstaking detail—the activities of one particular police battalion, detailing its members' transformation from regular men into killers. Yet in doing so, he hopes to show that this could happen to any of us. These men were, after all, "ordinary." Many men in similar situations, from Japan to Vietnam to the more recent prison camp of Abu Ghraib* in Iraq, have acted in similar ways. Browning suggests that the potential for this evil exists within each of us. His work is a classic, because it combines the methods of the historian, the understanding of the social psychologist, and the clarity of a moralist.

NOTES

1   Edward Westermann, "Shaping the Police Soldier as an Instrument for Annihilation," in *The Impact of Nazism: New Perspectives on the Third Reich and Its Legacy*, eds. Alan E. Steinweis and Daniel E. Rogers (Lincoln, NE: University of Nebraska Press, 2003), 129–50.

2   Timothy Snyder, *Bloodlands: Europe between Hitler and Stalin* (New York: Basic Books, 2000).

3   Jan Gross, *Fear: Anti-Semitism in Poland after Auschwitz. An Essay in Historical Interpretation* (Princeton, NJ: Princeton University Press, 2006).

4   Robert Gellately, *Backing Hitler: Consent and Coercion in Nazi Germany* (Oxford: Oxford University Press, 2001); Jill Stephenson, *Hitler's Home Front: Württemberg under the Nazis* (London: Bloomsbury, 2006).

5   Dan Stone, "Holocaust Historiography and Cultural History," in *The Holocaust and Historical Methodology* (New York: Bergahan, 2012), 56.

6   Christopher R. Browning, *Ordinary Men: Reserve Police Battalion 101 and the Final Solution in Poland* (London: Penguin, 2001), 146.

7   Jeffrey Herf, *Divided Memory: Nazi Past in the Two Germanys* (Cambridge, MA: Harvard University Press, 1997).

8   Eric Johnson and Karl-Heinz Reuband, *What We Knew: Terror, Mass Murder and Everyday Life in Nazi Germany. An Oral History* (London and New York: John Murray, 2005).

GLOSSARY

GLOSSARY OF TERMS

Abu Ghraib: a prison in Iraq that was used by United States forces after their invasion of that country in 2003. In 2004, it became apparent that military personnel had been torturing and abusing prisoners there, which caused a major scandal.

Anti-Semitism: refers to a prejudice against Jews as a people. Anti-Semitism is often distinguished from anti-Judaism, which discriminates against Jews on the basis of their religious beliefs.

Auschwitz-Birkenau: a combined labor and extermination camp, situated at Auschwitz, near Krakow in Poland, where 1.1 million Jews were murdered.

Belzec: one of the Nazi extermination camps built in occupied Poland, near Lublin, in late 1941.

Chelmno: one of the Nazi extermination camps built in occupied Poland, near Lodz, in late 1941. It was at Chelmno that the Nazis pioneered the method of murder in gas vans.

Civil Rights Movement: a movement that developed out of the United States in the 1950s and 1960s and aimed at ending the institutional discrimination and segregation imposed on African American communities. The movement was led by charismatic figures like Dr. Martin Luther King, who mobilized a series of massive boycotts and marches.

Cold War: a term that refers to the confrontation between the two superpowers, the United States and the Soviet Union, that began after the end of World War II and lasted until the collapse of the Soviet

Union in 1991. It was a conflict that stopped short of direct conflict, but involved an arms race, propaganda, invasions of neighboring states, and proxy wars.

Communism: an ideology that aims to abolish private property, put an end to capitalism, and create an egalitarian society. Communism was the official system of the Soviet Union.

Comparative history: the comparison of different peoples and societies, most often during the same era, but sometimes when they share cultural similarities.

Concentration camp: a camp where non-military, perceived enemies of the state are detained in poor conditions and often without trial. Generally associated with the Nazi regime in World War II, where camps held Jews and other persecuted minorities such as homosexuals, gypsies, and communists, using them to provide forced labor. Detainees were later executed in large numbers.

Democratic Party: one of the two major United States political parties alongside the Republican Party. It favors a liberal approach, supporting social and economic equality and some government intervention.

Eastern Front: a World War II term referring to German campaigns in the east of Europe. First there was the invasion of Poland in 1939, followed by the invasion of the Soviet Union (Operation Barbarossa) in the summer of 1941. The drive east saw not just huge military losses on the battlefield, but also the systematic murder of civilians.

Final Solution: a synonym for the Holocaust. The Nazi Party upper echelons explicitly conceived of the Holocaust as the "Final solution to the Jewish problem."

Führer: the official title of Adolf Hitler as "supreme leader" of the Third Reich.

Functionalism: a term used to describe a particular point of view in understanding how the Holocaust happened. In the debate over the origins of the Holocaust in the 1970s and 1980s, functionalist historians such as Hans Mommsen tended to emphasize that there was nothing inevitable about the genocide. Rather, it emerged as a policy in response to specific structural problems in the Nazi regime; this could be the mass of annexed new territory during the war, or the radicalization caused by competing government departments.

Genocide: the systematic and deliberate destruction of a racial or ethnic group. Aside from the Holocaust, famous other genocides include the killing of Armenians during World War I and attempted eliminations in Rwanda in the 1990s.

Ghetto: a residential area reserved for Jewish communities, in which access was strictly controlled, established first in early modern Europe. The Nazis created ghettos in many conquered Eastern European cities (such as Warsaw and Lodz in Poland), in which Jewish populations were forced to live, often in dreadful conditions.

Historikerstreit: literally translated as the "historians' quarrel," the term refers to a fierce controversy in German scholarship in the 1980s. It was triggered by the work of Ernst Nolte, who claimed that the Holocaust needed to be seen as a defensive move against the feared killing of Germans by the Soviet Union. Nolte also urged historians to try to feel empathy for the German soldiers fighting on the Eastern Front and to try to see the war through their eyes.

Holocaust: refers to the systematic murder of around six million Jews and other persecuted minorities in Europe by Nazi Germany and her allies. When exactly the Holocaust began remains a subject of great controversy, but most historians agree that the majority of the killing occurred in the years 1941–5.

Ideology: a set of firmly held beliefs that are used to underpin political and social theories.

Intentionalism: a term used to describe a particular point of view in understanding how the Holocaust happened. In the debate over the origins of the Holocaust in the 1970s and 1980s, intentionalist historians tended to stress that the destruction of the Jews was a key part of the plan of Nazi leaders from the beginning. So the Holocaust came out of the ideology of Hitler and his unwavering objective—to solve the "Jewish question."

Jews: a follower of the religion of Judaism and member of the Semitic community descended from the ancient Hebrew people of Israel.

Jósefów: a village in Poland where German Reserve Police Battalion 101 carried out their first massacre. The men of the village were transported to Lublin for forced labor, but the women, children, and elderly were shot on the spot. Discussion of the event forms a key chapter in Browning's analysis.

Microhistory: an approach to history that has become increasingly popular since the 1970s and the pioneering work of Italian historian Carlo Ginzburg. Microhistories aim to provide a rich reconstruction of one particular incident or character to illuminate broader themes.

My Lai Massacre: the most notorious American atrocity of the Vietnam War that occurred in the village of My Lai in March 1968 and saw the rape and murder of between 350 and 500 Vietnamese villagers. None of the perpetrators, other than the commander William Calley, was ever brought to justice.

Nazi Party: a commonly used name for the NSDAP— the National Socialist German Workers' Party—that was led by Adolf Hitler and ruled Germany between 1933 and 1945.

Ordnungspolizei (**"Order Police"**): the reserve forces who were drafted and deployed in Nazi-occupied Poland. One of the major insights of Browning's book is the role such units played in trying to implement the Final Solution.

Pacific War: The conflicts that formed a part of World War II, primarily fought out between the Allied Powers and the Empire of Japan. The conflict took place in the Pacific and East Asia and lasted from 1941 to 1945.

Polemical: A stong written or verbal attack.

Republican Party: one of the two major United States political parties alongside the Democratic Party. It favors a conservative approach supporting free-market economy and limited government.

Reserve Police Battalion 101: a battalion made up of men who were predominantly middle-aged and working-class Germans— "ordinary men"—who were either too old for the army or who volunteered to gain exemption from a military draft. They took part in genocidal "special actions" in Nazi-occupied Poland.

Reunification of Germany: the 1990 reuniting of West and East Germany following the collapse of communism in the eastern part of Europe.

Sobibor: one of the extermination camps built by the Nazis in occupied Poland, near Lublin, in 1942.

Social history: refers to an approach in history that seeks to analyze not the political elite, but the broader mass of society. Social historians have been notable for their work on class, gender roles, and everyday life.

Sonderweg: a German term for "special path," first used by late nineteenth-century German conservatives, before being co-opted by historians such as Hans-Ulrich Wehler to describe the origins of Germany's turn to militarism and violence in the twentieth century.

Soviet Union: a communist state that existed from 1922 to 1991 based on principles of Marxist-Leninism (the idea of trying to implement communism using a dictatorship). Its territory encompassed Russia and surrounding states in Eastern Europe and Central Asia.

Third Reich: the common English name given to refer to the period of Nazi Party rule in Germany under Adolf Hitler, which lasted from 1933 to 1945.

Trawnikis: the name given to Ukrainian, Lithuanian, and Latvian volunteers who were chosen to act as auxiliaries to the Nazi police. They were selected for their anti-communist and anti-Semitic views, although many joined out of a desire to avoid starvation and escape serving on the Eastern Front.

Treblinka: one of the Nazi extermination camps in occupied Poland, built in the summer of 1942.

Vietnam War: a complex international conflict that lasted from 1955 to 1975 and pitted American forces against Vietnamese communists, backed by China and other nations. The war was designed to halt the spread of communism, but it was a highly controversial conflict that caused many divisions, especially between the young and those in power in the United States.

Watergate: the name of a building in Washington, DC in the United States, and containing the national headquarters of the Democratic Party, which was burgled on June 17, 1972 by persons connected with the Republican administration. "Watergate" became the umbrella term for the 1972–3 scandal that brought down the presidency of Richard Nixon.

Weather Underground: also known as the Weathermen, this was a radical group founded in Michigan, United States in the late 1960s, undertaking a campaign of subversion and bombings aimed at overthrowing the American government.

Wehrmacht: the name given to the German armed forces during World War II. Recent scholarship has shown that there was involvement of supposedly apolitical military forces in genocidal operations.

Yad Vashem: the museum of the Holocaust in Jerusalem, Israel. It has unrivalled collections and is involved in sponsoring new scholarship on the subject and in spreading Holocaust education.

World War II (1939–45): a global conflict fought between the Axis Powers (Germany, Italy, and Japan) and the victorious Allied Powers (the United Kingdom and its colonies, the Soviet Union, and the United States).

PEOPLE MENTIONED IN THE TEXT

Andrej Angrick (b. 1962) is a German historian interested in the Holocaust and German war crimes. He has published an important study of the persecution of Jews in Latvia.

Hannah Arendt (1906–75) was a German Jewish philosopher and historian who fled Nazi Germany and emigrated to America. One of the greatest post-war intellectuals, she wrote the seminal books *Origins of Totalitarianism* (1951) and *Eichmann in Jerusalem* (1963), from which the famous phrase "banality of evil" derives.

Omer Bartov (b. 1953) is an Israeli-born historian who is professor of European history at Brown University in the United States. He has written widely on Jewish life in Galicia and the atrocities carried out by the regular German army, the Wehrmacht.

Werner Best (1903–89) was a jurist, police chief, and Nazi Party leader from Darmstadt, who was instrumental in bringing anti-Jewish measures to Denmark.

Martin Broszat (1926–89) was a leading German historian of the Third Reich. He held many professorships and positions, the most important of which was his leadership of the Institute of Contemporary History in Munich.

Alon Confino is an Israeli-born professor of history who has published widely on memory cultures in Germany, issues of historical method, and the cultural and ideological roots of anti-Semitism—what he calls the fantasy of a "world without Jews."

John Dower (b. 1938) is a Pulitzer Prize-winning historian, and is currently a professor at the Massachusetts Institute of Technology. He is the author of *War without Mercy* (1988), which documented American war crimes in the Pacific during World War II.

Adolf Eichmann (1906–62) was a lieutenant-colonel in the SS who was charged with organizing the transport of Jews to ghettos and camps in Nazi-occupied Eastern Europe. Having fled to Argentina after the war, he was captured by Israeli security forces, tried for war crimes in Israel, and executed.

Geoff Eley (b. 1949) is professor of history at the University of Michigan, and one of the foremost left-wing historians of the German Second Empire. In *The Crooked Line* (2005) he traced the changing fortunes of social history.

General Francisco Franco (1892–1975) was the right-wing dictator of Spain after seizing power in the wake of the Spanish Civil War in 1939. He remained in control of the country until his death in 1975.

Peter Fritzsche (b. 1959) is a professor of history at the University of Illinois. As well as writings on historical memory and the city of Berlin, he is one of the most respected historians of Nazi Germany, focusing on the cultures of consent in daily life.

Robert Gellately (b. 1943) is Canadian-born historian who is professor at Florida University and a specialist on European history during World War II and the Cold War.

Daniel Jonah Goldhagen (b. 1959) is an American historian and journalist, most famous for a number of studies of Nazi Germany and the Holocaust, which he wrote while a professor of government at Harvard University.

Jan Gross (b. 1943) is professor of history and sociology at Princeton University, and author of acclaimed and controversial books about the Polish role in anti-Semitic violence during and after World War II.

Ulrich Herbert (b. 1951) is a distinguished historian at the University of Freiburg.

Raul Hilberg (1928–2007) was an Austrian Jewish historian and political scientist who emigrated to America with his family in 1939 and served in the American army. He wrote the first studies on the Holocaust after World War II at a time when the subject was barely appreciated.

Heinrich Himmler (1900–45) was a leading member of the Nazi Party and head of the SS. He had a decisive role in ordering the extermination of Jews in Eastern Europe and pushing ahead with the Final Solution.

Adolf Hitler (1889–1945) was the Austrian-born leader of the Nazi Party, who became Chancellor of Germany in 1933. Dismantling all opposition, Hitler set himself up as dictator, before his expansionist policies led to World War II. This led to the total defeat and destruction of his regime in 1945.

David Irving (b. 1938) is a British author and historian, notorious for his views on Adolf Hitler and widely recognized as a Holocaust denier. At a landmark libel case in 1997, numerous historians, including Christopher Browning, came to testify against Irving and his distortions.

Eric Johnson (b. 1948) is professor of history at Central Michigan University and a member of the Institute for Advanced Study in Princeton. He has published important works on urban culture, the Nazi Terror, and Nazi memory.

Sir Ian Kershaw (b. 1943) is a British historian who is acknowledged as one of the world's foremost experts on the Nazi regime and has written a number of in-depth studies of Hitler.

Peter Longerich (b. 1955) is a German professor and historian. He is a leading expert in the study of the Holocaust, and has written an acclaimed biography of Heinrich Himmler.

David Mandel (b. 1966) is a Canadian sociologist who has held positions at York University and the University of Toronto.

Michael Mann (b. 1942) is a sociology professor at the University of California, Los Angeles. He has argued for taking a longer-term view on Nazi violence by reconstructing the histories of members of the police battalions.

Michael Marrus (b. 1941) is professor emeritus of Holocaust Studies at the University of Toronto. He has written widely on refugees in the interwar period, and on French Jews from the Dreyfus affair down to Vichy.

Jürgen Matthäus (b. 1959) is currently a director of the United States Holocaust Memorial Museum, and has worked with Browning on numerous occasions.

Mark Mazower (b. 1958) is a British historian of modern Europe. He has written extensively about the Third Reich, most recently in

Hitler's Empire: Nazi Rule in Occupied Europe (2008). He teaches at Columbia University in the United States.

Stanley Milgram (1933–84) was an American social psychologist, most famous for the so-called "Milgram experiments," which purported to prove that human beings would naturally commit acts of terrible violence if instructed to do so by men of authority.

Hans Mommsen (b. 1930) is a left-wing German historian of the Nazi period and the German working class. He was the foremost exponent of a functionalist interpretation of Nazi racial policy.

Richard Nixon (1913–94) was one of the most controversial of American presidents. Nixon led the Republican Party to victory in 1968 and 1972. Crucial policies of his administration included rapprochement with Communist China and ending the war in Vietnam, but he was mired in scandal after the Watergate affair and resigned from office in 1974.

Walter Reich is professor of international affairs and psychiatry at the Elliott School at George Washington University. He was former director of the US Holocaust Memorial Museum.

Timothy Snyder (b. 1969) is an American historian and the author of *Bloodlands: Europe between Hitler and Stalin* (2010). He teaches at Yale University in the United States.

Dan Stone (b. 1971) is a British historian. He has written widely on the historiography of the Holocaust, the liberation of the death camps, and the emergence of a new Europe after 1945.

Wilhelm Trapp (1889–1948) was a career policeman and commander of the Reserve Police Battalion 101, with whom he undertook genocidal "special actions" against Jews in Nazi-occupied Poland. After the war he was arrested by the British and extradited to Poland, where he was executed in 1948 for crimes against Polish citizens, rather than against Jews.

James Waller (b. 1961) is currently the Cohen Chair of Holocaust and Genocide Studies at Keene State College in the United States.

Harald Welzer (b. 1958) is a professor of social psychology at the University of Flensburg.

WORKS CITED

WORKS CITED

Angrick, Andrej. *Besatzungspolitik und Massenmord: Die Einsatzgruppe D in der südlichen Sowjetunion 1941–1943*. Hamburg: Hamburger Edition, 2003.

Bartov, Omer. *Murder in Our Midst: The Holocaust, Industrial Killing, and Representation*. New York: Oxford University Press, 1996.

Bauer, Yehuda. *A History of the Holocaust*. New York: F. Watts, 1982.

Bauman, Zygmunt. *Modernity and the Holocaust*. Cambridge: Polity, 1989.

Browder, George C. "Perpetrator Character and Motivation: An Emerging Consensus." *Holocaust and Genocide Studies* 17, no. 3 (2003): 480–97.

Browning, Christopher R. *Every Day Lasts a Year: A Jewish Family's Correspondence from Poland*. Cambridge: Cambridge University Press, 2007.

The Final Solution and the German Foreign Office: A Study of Referat D III of Abteilung Deutschland, 1940–1943. New York: Holmes & Meier, 1978.

Nazi Policy, Jewish Workers, German Killers. Cambridge: Cambridge

University Press, 2000.

Ordinary Men: Reserve Police Battalion 101 and the Final Solution in Poland. London: Penguin, 2001 [1992].

The Origins of the Final Solution: The Evolution of Nazi Jewish Policy, September 1939–March 1942. Lincoln, NE: University of Nebraska Press, 2004.

Remembering Survival: Inside a Nazi Slave-Labor Camp. New York: Norton, 2010.

Confino, Alon. *A World Without Jews: The Nazi Imagination from*

Persecution to Genocide. New Haven, CT and London: Yale University Press, 2014.

Dower, John. *War without Mercy: Race and Power in the Pacific War*. New York: Pantheon Books, 1986.

Eley, Geoff. *Nazism as Fascism: Violence, Ideology and the Ground of Consent in Germany 1930–1945*. London and New York: Routledge, 2013.

Friedländer, Saul. *Probing the Limits of Representation: Nazism and the Final Solution*. Cambridge, MA: Harvard University Press, 1992.

Fritzsche, Peter. *Germans into Nazis*. Cambridge, MA: Cambridge University Press, 1998.

Gellately, Robert. *Backing Hitler: Consent and Coercion in Nazi Germany*. Oxford: Oxford University Press, 2001.

Ginzburg, Carlo. *The Cheese and the Worms: The Cosmos of a Sixteenth-Century Miller*. Translated by John and Anne Tedeschi. Baltimore, MD: Johns Hopkins University Press, 1980.

Goldhagen, Daniel Jonah. "The Evil of Banality." *The New Republic*, July 13, 1992: 49–52.

Hitler's Willing Executioners: Ordinary Germans and the Holocaust. New York: Vintage, 1997.

Goldhagen, Daniel J., Christopher R. Browning, and Leon Wieseltier. *The "Willing Executioners"/"Ordinary Men" Debate: Selections from the Symposium*. Washington, DC: United States Holocaust Research Institute, 1996.

Gross, Jan. *Neighbors: The Destruction of the Jewish Community in Jedwabne, Poland*. Princeton, NJ: Princeton University Press, 2001.

Fear: Anti-Semitism in Poland after Auschwitz: An Essay in

Historical Interpretation. Princeton, NJ: Princeton University Press, 2006.

Guttenplan, D. D. *The Holocaust on Trial*. New York: Norton, 2001.

Herbert, Ulrich. *Best: Biographische Studien über Radikalismus, Weltanschauung, und Vernunft, 1903–89*. Bonn: J. H. W. Diet, 1996.

Herf, Jeffrey. *Divided Memory: Nazi Past in the Two Germanys*. Cambridge,

MA: Harvard University Press, 1997.

Hilberg, Raul. *The Destruction of the European Jews* (3rd ed.), Vol. 3. New Haven, CT: Yale University Press, 2003.

Hitler, Adolf. *Mein Kampf*. 2 vols. Munich: Franz Eher Nachfolger, 1925–6.

Jäckel, Eberhard, and Jürgen Rohwer, eds. *Der Mord an den Judem im Zweiten Weltkrieg: Entschlußbildung und Verwirklichung*. Stuttgart: Deutsche Verlag-Anstalt, 1985.

Johnson, Eric. *Nazi Terror: The Gestapo, Jews and Ordinary Germans*. New York: Basic Books, 2000.

Johnson, Eric, and Karl-Heinz Reuband. *What We Knew: Terror, Mass Murder and Everyday Life in Nazi Germany. An Oral History*. London and New York: John Murray, 2005.

Longerich, Peter. *Heinrich Himmler: Biographie*. Munich: Siedler, 2008.

Holocaust: The Nazi Persecution and Murder of the Jews. Oxford: Oxford University Press, 2010.

Mandel, David. "The Obedience Alibi: Milgram's Account of the Holocaust Reconsidered." *Analyse & Kritik* 20 (1998): 74–94.

Mann, Michael. "Were the Perpetrators of Genocide 'Ordinary Men' or 'Real Nazis'? Results from Fifteen Hundred Biographies." *Journal of Genocide Studies* 14 (2000): 331–66.

Marrus, Michael. *The Holocaust in History*. Toronto: Key Porter Books, 2000.

Matthäus, Jürgen. "Controlled Escalation: Himmler's Men in the Summer of 1941 and the Holocaust in the Occupied Soviet Territories." *Holocaust and Genocide Studies* 21, no. 2 (2007): 218–42.

Mazower, Mark. *Hitler's Empire: Nazi Rule in Occupied Europe*. London: Allen Lane, 2008.

"Violence and the State in the Twentieth Century." *American Historical Review* 107 (2002): 1147–67.

Midlarsky, Manus. *The Killing Trap: Genocide in the Twentieth Century*. Cambridge: Cambridge University Press, 2005.

Mommsen, Hans. "Cumulative Radicalisation and Progressive Self-Destruction as Structural Determinants of the Nazi Dictatorship." In *Stalinism and Nazism: Dictatorships in Comparison*, edited by Ian Kershaw and Moshe Lewin, 75–87. Cambridge: Cambridge University Press, 1997.

Moses, A.D. "Structure and Agency in the Holocaust: Daniel J. Goldhagen and His Critics." *History and Theory* 37, no. 2 (1998): 194–219.

Orne, Martin T., and Charles H. Holland. "On the Ecological Validity of Laboratory Deceptions." *International Journal of Psychiatry* 6 (1968): 282–93.

Preston, Paul. *The Spanish Holocaust: Inquisition and Extermination in Twentieth-century Spain*. London: HarperCollins, 2012.

Reich, Walter. "The Men Who Pulled the Trigger." *New York Times*, April 12, 1992.

Reicher, Stephen, and S. Alexander Haslam. "Obedience: Revisiting Milgram's Shock Experiments." In *Social Psychology: Revisiting the Classic Studies*, edited by Joanne R. Smith and S. Alexander Aslam, 106–25. London: Sage, 2012.

Shatz, Adam. "Browning's Version: A Mild-Mannered Historian's Quest to Understand the Perpetrators of the Holocaust." *Lingua Franca* 7, no. 2 (February 1997): 48–57.

Snyder, Timothy. *Bloodlands: Europe between Hitler and Stalin*. New York: Basic

Books, 2000.

Stephenson, Jill. *Hitler's Home Front: Württemberg under the Nazis*. London: Bloomsbury, 2006.

Stone, Dan. "Holocaust Historiography and Cultural History." In *The Holocaust and Historical Methodology*, 44–60. New York: Bergahan, 2012.

Waller, James. *Becoming Evil: How Ordinary People Commit Genocide and Mass Killing*. New York: Oxford University Press, 2002.

Westermann, Edward. "Shaping the Police Soldier as an Instrument for Annihilation." In *The Impact of Nazism: New Perspectives on the Third Reich and Its Legacy*, edited by Alan E. Steinweis and Daniel E. Rogers, 129–50. Lincoln, NE: University of Nebraska Press, 2003.

THE MACAT LIBRARY
BY DISCIPLINE

AFRICANA STUDIES

Chinua Achebe's *An Image of Africa: Racism in Conrad's Heart of Darkness*
W. E. B. Du Bois's *The Souls of Black Folk*
Zora Neale Huston's *Characteristics of Negro Expression*
Martin Luther King Jr's *Why We Can't Wait*
Toni Morrison's *Playing in the Dark: Whiteness in the American Literary Imagination*

ANTHROPOLOGY

Arjun Appadurai's *Modernity at Large: Cultural Dimensions of Globalisation*
Philippe Ariès's *Centuries of Childhood*
Franz Boas's *Race, Language and Culture*
Kim Chan & Renée Mauborgne's *Blue Ocean Strategy*
Jared Diamond's *Guns, Germs & Steel: the Fate of Human Societies*
Jared Diamond's *Collapse: How Societies Choose to Fail or Survive*
E. E. Evans-Pritchard's *Witchcraft, Oracles and Magic Among the Azande*
James Ferguson's *The Anti-Politics Machine*
Clifford Geertz's *The Interpretation of Cultures*
David Graeber's *Debt: the First 5000 Years*
Karen Ho's *Liquidated: An Ethnography of Wall Street*
Geert Hofstede's *Culture's Consequences: Comparing Values, Behaviors, Institutes and Organizations across Nations*
Claude Lévi-Strauss's *Structural Anthropology*
Jay Macleod's *Ain't No Makin' It: Aspirations and Attainment in a Low-Income Neighborhood*
Saba Mahmood's *The Politics of Piety: The Islamic Revival and the Feminist Subjec*t
Marcel Mauss's *The Gift*

BUSINESS

Jean Lave & Etienne Wenger's *Situated Learning*
Theodore Levitt's *Marketing Myopia*
Burton G. Malkiel's *A Random Walk Down Wall Street*
Douglas McGregor's *The Human Side of Enterprise*
Michael Porter's *Competitive Strategy: Creating and Sustaining Superior Performance*
John Kotter's *Leading Change*
C. K. Prahalad & Gary Hamel's *The Core Competence of the Corporation*

CRIMINOLOGY

Michelle Alexander's *The New Jim Crow: Mass Incarceration in the Age of Colorblindness*
Michael R. Gottfredson & Travis Hirschi's *A General Theory of Crime*
Richard Herrnstein & Charles A. Murray's *The Bell Curve: Intelligence and Class Structure in American Life*
Elizabeth Loftus's *Eyewitness Testimony*
Jay Macleod's *Ain't No Makin' It: Aspirations and Attainment in a Low-Income Neighborhood*
Philip Zimbardo's *The Lucifer Effect*

ECONOMICS

Janet Abu-Lughod's *Before European Hegemony*
Ha-Joon Chang's *Kicking Away the Ladder*
David Brion Davis's *The Problem of Slavery in the Age of Revolution*
Milton Friedman's *The Role of Monetary Policy*
Milton Friedman's *Capitalism and Freedom*
David Graeber's *Debt: the First 5000 Years*
Friedrich Hayek's *The Road to Serfdom*
Karen Ho's *Liquidated: An Ethnography of Wall Street*

The Macat Library By Discipline

John Maynard Keynes's *The General Theory of Employment, Interest and Money*
Charles P. Kindleberger's *Manias, Panics and Crashes*
Robert Lucas's *Why Doesn't Capital Flow from Rich to Poor Countries?*
Burton G. Malkiel's *A Random Walk Down Wall Street*
Thomas Robert Malthus's *An Essay on the Principle of Population*
Karl Marx's *Capital*
Thomas Piketty's *Capital in the Twenty-First Century*
Amartya Sen's *Development as Freedom*
Adam Smith's *The Wealth of Nations*
Nassim Nicholas Taleb's *The Black Swan: The Impact of the Highly Improbable*
Amos Tversky's & Daniel Kahneman's *Judgment under Uncertainty: Heuristics and Biases*
Mahbub Ul Haq's *Reflections on Human Development*
Max Weber's *The Protestant Ethic and the Spirit of Capitalism*

FEMINISM AND GENDER STUDIES

Judith Butler's *Gender Trouble*
Simone De Beauvoir's *The Second Sex*
Michel Foucault's *History of Sexuality*
Betty Friedan's *The Feminine Mystique*
Saba Mahmood's *The Politics of Piety: The Islamic Revival and the Feminist Subject*
Joan Wallach Scott's *Gender and the Politics of History*
Mary Wollstonecraft's *A Vindication of the Rights of Woman*
Virginia Woolf's *A Room of One's Own*

GEOGRAPHY

The Brundtland Report's *Our Common Future*
Rachel Carson's *Silent Spring*
Charles Darwin's *On the Origin of Species*
James Ferguson's *The Anti-Politics Machine*
Jane Jacobs's *The Death and Life of Great American Cities*
James Lovelock's *Gaia: A New Look at Life on Earth*
Amartya Sen's *Development as Freedom*
Mathis Wackernagel & William Rees's *Our Ecological Footprint*

HISTORY

Janet Abu-Lughod's *Before European Hegemony*
Benedict Anderson's *Imagined Communities*
Bernard Bailyn's *The Ideological Origins of the American Revolution*
Hanna Batatu's *The Old Social Classes And The Revolutionary Movements Of Iraq*
Christopher Browning's *Ordinary Men: Reserve Police Batallion 101 and the Final Solution in Poland*
Edmund Burke's *Reflections on the Revolution in France*
William Cronon's *Nature's Metropolis: Chicago And The Great West*
Alfred W. Crosby's *The Columbian Exchange*
Hamid Dabashi's *Iran: A People Interrupted*
David Brion Davis's *The Problem of Slavery in the Age of Revolution*
Nathalie Zemon Davis's *The Return of Martin Guerre*
Jared Diamond's *Guns, Germs & Steel: the Fate of Human Societies*
Frank Dikotter's *Mao's Great Famine*
John W Dower's *War Without Mercy: Race And Power In The Pacific War*
W. E. B. Du Bois's *The Souls of Black Folk*
Richard J. Evans's *In Defence of History*
Lucien Febvre's *The Problem of Unbelief in the 16th Century*
Sheila Fitzpatrick's *Everyday Stalinism*

Eric Foner's *Reconstruction: America's Unfinished Revolution, 1863-1877*
Michel Foucault's *Discipline and Punish*
Michel Foucault's *History of Sexuality*
Francis Fukuyama's *The End of History and the Last Man*
John Lewis Gaddis's *We Now Know: Rethinking Cold War History*
Ernest Gellner's *Nations and Nationalism*
Eugene Genovese's *Roll, Jordan, Roll: The World the Slaves Made*
Carlo Ginzburg's *The Night Battles*
Daniel Goldhagen's *Hitler's Willing Executioners*
Jack Goldstone's *Revolution and Rebellion in the Early Modern World*
Antonio Gramsci's *The Prison Notebooks*
Alexander Hamilton, John Jay & James Madison's *The Federalist Papers*
Christopher Hill's *The World Turned Upside Down*
Carole Hillenbrand's *The Crusades: Islamic Perspectives*
Thomas Hobbes's *Leviathan*
Eric Hobsbawm's *The Age Of Revolution*
John A. Hobson's *Imperialism: A Study*
Albert Hourani's *History of the Arab Peoples*
Samuel P. Huntington's *The Clash of Civilizations and the Remaking of World Order*
C. L. R. James's *The Black Jacobins*
Tony Judt's *Postwar: A History of Europe Since 1945*
Ernst Kantorowicz's *The King's Two Bodies: A Study in Medieval Political Theology*
Paul Kennedy's *The Rise and Fall of the Great Powers*
Ian Kershaw's *The "Hitler Myth": Image and Reality in the Third Reich*
John Maynard Keynes's *The General Theory of Employment, Interest and Money*
Charles P. Kindleberger's *Manias, Panics and Crashes*
Martin Luther King Jr's *Why We Can't Wait*
Henry Kissinger's *World Order: Reflections on the Character of Nations and the Course of History*
Thomas Kuhn's *The Structure of Scientific Revolutions*
Georges Lefebvre's *The Coming of the French Revolution*
John Locke's *Two Treatises of Government*
Niccolò Machiavelli's *The Prince*
Thomas Robert Malthus's *An Essay on the Principle of Population*
Mahmood Mamdani's *Citizen and Subject: Contemporary Africa And The Legacy Of Late Colonialism*
Karl Marx's *Capital*
Stanley Milgram's *Obedience to Authority*
John Stuart Mill's *On Liberty*
Thomas Paine's *Common Sense*
Thomas Paine's *Rights of Man*
Geoffrey Parker's *Global Crisis: War, Climate Change and Catastrophe in the Seventeenth Century*
Jonathan Riley-Smith's *The First Crusade and the Idea of Crusading*
Jean-Jacques Rousseau's *The Social Contract*
Joan Wallach Scott's *Gender and the Politics of History*
Theda Skocpol's *States and Social Revolutions*
Adam Smith's *The Wealth of Nations*
Timothy Snyder's *Bloodlands: Europe Between Hitler and Stalin*
Sun Tzu's *The Art of War*
Keith Thomas's *Religion and the Decline of Magic*
Thucydides's *The History of the Peloponnesian War*
Frederick Jackson Turner's *The Significance of the Frontier in American History*
Odd Arne Westad's *The Global Cold War: Third World Interventions And The Making Of Our Times*

The Macat Library By Discipline

LITERATURE

Chinua Achebe's *An Image of Africa: Racism in Conrad's Heart of Darkness*
Roland Barthes's *Mythologies*
Homi K. Bhabha's *The Location of Culture*
Judith Butler's *Gender Trouble*
Simone De Beauvoir's *The Second Sex*
Ferdinand De Saussure's *Course in General Linguistics*
T. S. Eliot's *The Sacred Wood: Essays on Poetry and Criticism*
Zora Neale Huston's *Characteristics of Negro Expression*
Toni Morrison's *Playing in the Dark: Whiteness in the American Literary Imagination*
Edward Said's *Orientalism*
Gayatri Chakravorty Spivak's *Can the Subaltern Speak?*
Mary Wollstonecraft's *A Vindication of the Rights of Women*
Virginia Woolf's *A Room of One's Own*

PHILOSOPHY

Elizabeth Anscombe's *Modern Moral Philosophy*
Hannah Arendt's *The Human Condition*
Aristotle's *Metaphysics*
Aristotle's *Nicomachean Ethics*
Edmund Gettier's *Is Justified True Belief Knowledge?*
Georg Wilhelm Friedrich Hegel's *Phenomenology of Spirit*
David Hume's *Dialogues Concerning Natural Religion*
David Hume's *The Enquiry for Human Understanding*
Immanuel Kant's *Religion within the Boundaries of Mere Reason*
Immanuel Kant's *Critique of Pure Reason*
Søren Kierkegaard's *The Sickness Unto Death*
Søren Kierkegaard's *Fear and Trembling*
C. S. Lewis's *The Abolition of Man*
Alasdair MacIntyre's *After Virtue*
Marcus Aurelius's *Meditations*
Friedrich Nietzsche's *On the Genealogy of Morality*
Friedrich Nietzsche's *Beyond Good and Evil*
Plato's *Republic*
Plato's *Symposium*
Jean-Jacques Rousseau's *The Social Contract*
Gilbert Ryle's *The Concept of Mind*
Baruch Spinoza's *Ethics*
Sun Tzu's *The Art of War*
Ludwig Wittgenstein's *Philosophical Investigations*

POLITICS

Benedict Anderson's *Imagined Communities*
Aristotle's *Politics*
Bernard Bailyn's *The Ideological Origins of the American Revolution*
Edmund Burke's *Reflections on the Revolution in France*
John C. Calhoun's *A Disquisition on Government*
Ha-Joon Chang's *Kicking Away the Ladder*
Hamid Dabashi's *Iran: A People Interrupted*
Hamid Dabashi's *Theology of Discontent: The Ideological Foundation of the Islamic Revolution in Iran*
Robert Dahl's *Democracy and its Critics*
Robert Dahl's *Who Governs?*
David Brion Davis's *The Problem of Slavery in the Age of Revolution*

Alexis De Tocqueville's *Democracy in America*
James Ferguson's *The Anti-Politics Machine*
Frank Dikotter's *Mao's Great Famine*
Sheila Fitzpatrick's *Everyday Stalinism*
Eric Foner's *Reconstruction: America's Unfinished Revolution, 1863-1877*
Milton Friedman's *Capitalism and Freedom*
Francis Fukuyama's *The End of History and the Last Man*
John Lewis Gaddis's *We Now Know: Rethinking Cold War History*
Ernest Gellner's *Nations and Nationalism*
David Graeber's *Debt: the First 5000 Years*
Antonio Gramsci's *The Prison Notebooks*
Alexander Hamilton, John Jay & James Madison's *The Federalist Papers*
Friedrich Hayek's *The Road to Serfdom*
Christopher Hill's *The World Turned Upside Down*
Thomas Hobbes's *Leviathan*
John A. Hobson's *Imperialism: A Study*
Samuel P. Huntington's *The Clash of Civilizations and the Remaking of World Order*
Tony Judt's *Postwar: A History of Europe Since 1945*
David C. Kang's *China Rising: Peace, Power and Order in East Asia*
Paul Kennedy's *The Rise and Fall of Great Powers*
Robert Keohane's *After Hegemony*
Martin Luther King Jr.'s *Why We Can't Wait*
Henry Kissinger's *World Order: Reflections on the Character of Nations and the Course of History*
John Locke's *Two Treatises of Government*
Niccolò Machiavelli's *The Prince*
Thomas Robert Malthus's *An Essay on the Principle of Population*
Mahmood Mamdani's *Citizen and Subject: Contemporary Africa And The Legacy Of Late Colonialism*
Karl Marx's *Capital*
John Stuart Mill's *On Liberty*
John Stuart Mill's *Utilitarianism*
Hans Morgenthau's *Politics Among Nations*
Thomas Paine's *Common Sense*
Thomas Paine's *Rights of Man*
Thomas Piketty's *Capital in the Twenty-First Century*
Robert D. Putnam's *Bowling Alone*
John Rawls's *Theory of Justice*
Jean-Jacques Rousseau's *The Social Contract*
Theda Skocpol's *States and Social Revolutions*
Adam Smith's *The Wealth of Nations*
Sun Tzu's *The Art of War*
Henry David Thoreau's *Civil Disobedience*
Thucydides's *The History of the Peloponnesian War*
Kenneth Waltz's *Theory of International Politics*
Max Weber's *Politics as a Vocation*
Odd Arne Westad's *The Global Cold War: Third World Interventions And The Making Of Our Times*

POSTCOLONIAL STUDIES

Roland Barthes's *Mythologies*
Frantz Fanon's *Black Skin, White Masks*
Homi K. Bhabha's *The Location of Culture*
Gustavo Gutiérrez's *A Theology of Liberation*
Edward Said's *Orientalism*
Gayatri Chakravorty Spivak's *Can the Subaltern Speak?*

PSYCHOLOGY

Gordon Allport's *The Nature of Prejudice*
Alan Baddeley & Graham Hitch's *Aggression: A Social Learning Analysis*
Albert Bandura's *Aggression: A Social Learning Analysis*
Leon Festinger's *A Theory of Cognitive Dissonance*
Sigmund Freud's *The Interpretation of Dreams*
Betty Friedan's *The Feminine Mystique*
Michael R. Gottfredson & Travis Hirschi's *A General Theory of Crime*
Eric Hoffer's *The True Believer: Thoughts on the Nature of Mass Movements*
William James's *Principles of Psychology*
Elizabeth Loftus's *Eyewitness Testimony*
A. H. Maslow's *A Theory of Human Motivation*
Stanley Milgram's *Obedience to Authority*
Steven Pinker's *The Better Angels of Our Nature*
Oliver Sacks's *The Man Who Mistook His Wife For a Hat*
Richard Thaler & Cass Sunstein's *Nudge: Improving Decisions About Health, Wealth and Happiness*
Amos Tversky's *Judgment under Uncertainty: Heuristics and Biases*
Philip Zimbardo's *The Lucifer Effect*

SCIENCE

Rachel Carson's *Silent Spring*
William Cronon's *Nature's Metropolis: Chicago And The Great West*
Alfred W. Crosby's *The Columbian Exchange*
Charles Darwin's *On the Origin of Species*
Richard Dawkin's *The Selfish Gene*
Thomas Kuhn's *The Structure of Scientific Revolutions*
Geoffrey Parker's *Global Crisis: War, Climate Change and Catastrophe in the Seventeenth Century*
Mathis Wackernagel & William Rees's *Our Ecological Footprint*

SOCIOLOGY

Michelle Alexander's *The New Jim Crow: Mass Incarceration in the Age of Colorblindness*
Gordon Allport's *The Nature of Prejudice*
Albert Bandura's *Aggression: A Social Learning Analysis*
Hanna Batatu's *The Old Social Classes And The Revolutionary Movements Of Iraq*
Ha-Joon Chang's *Kicking Away the Ladder*
W. E. B. Du Bois's *The Souls of Black Folk*
Émile Durkheim's *On Suicide*
Frantz Fanon's *Black Skin, White Masks*
Frantz Fanon's *The Wretched of the Earth*
Eric Foner's *Reconstruction: America's Unfinished Revolution, 1863-1877*
Eugene Genovese's *Roll, Jordan, Roll: The World the Slaves Made*
Jack Goldstone's *Revolution and Rebellion in the Early Modern World*
Antonio Gramsci's *The Prison Notebooks*
Richard Herrnstein & Charles A Murray's *The Bell Curve: Intelligence and Class Structure in American Life*
Eric Hoffer's *The True Believer: Thoughts on the Nature of Mass Movements*
Jane Jacobs's *The Death and Life of Great American Cities*
Robert Lucas's *Why Doesn't Capital Flow from Rich to Poor Countries?*
Jay Macleod's *Ain't No Makin' It: Aspirations and Attainment in a Low Income Neighborhood*
Elaine May's *Homeward Bound: American Families in the Cold War Era*
Douglas McGregor's *The Human Side of Enterprise*
C. Wright Mills's *The Sociological Imagination*

Thomas Piketty's *Capital in the Twenty-First Century*
Robert D. Putman's *Bowling Alone*
David Riesman's *The Lonely Crowd: A Study of the Changing American Character*
Edward Said's *Orientalism*
Joan Wallach Scott's *Gender and the Politics of History*
Theda Skocpol's *States and Social Revolutions*
Max Weber's *The Protestant Ethic and the Spirit of Capitalism*

THEOLOGY

Augustine's *Confessions*
Benedict's *Rule of St Benedict*
Gustavo Gutiérrez's *A Theology of Liberation*
Carole Hillenbrand's *The Crusades: Islamic Perspectives*
David Hume's *Dialogues Concerning Natural Religion*
Immanuel Kant's *Religion within the Boundaries of Mere Reason*
Ernst Kantorowicz's *The King's Two Bodies: A Study in Medieval Political Theology*
Søren Kierkegaard's *The Sickness Unto Death*
C. S. Lewis's *The Abolition of Man*
Saba Mahmood's *The Politics of Piety: The Islamic Revival and the Feminist Subject*
Baruch Spinoza's *Ethics*
Keith Thomas's *Religion and the Decline of Magic*

COMING SOON

Chris Argyris's *The Individual and the Organisation*
Seyla Benhabib's *The Rights of Others*
Walter Benjamin's *The Work Of Art in the Age of Mechanical Reproduction*
John Berger's *Ways of Seeing*
Pierre Bourdieu's *Outline of a Theory of Practice*
Mary Douglas's *Purity and Danger*
Roland Dworkin's *Taking Rights Seriously*
James G. March's *Exploration and Exploitation in Organisational Learning*
Ikujiro Nonaka's *A Dynamic Theory of Organizational Knowledge Creation*
Griselda Pollock's *Vision and Difference*
Amartya Sen's *Inequality Re-Examined*
Susan Sontag's *On Photography*
Yasser Tabbaa's *The Transformation of Islamic Art*
Ludwig von Mises's *Theory of Money and Credit*

Macat Disciplines

Access the greatest ideas and thinkers across entire disciplines, including

Postcolonial Studies

Roland Barthes's *Mythologies*
Frantz Fanon's *Black Skin, White Masks*
Homi K. Bhabha's *The Location of Culture*
Gustavo Gutiérrez's *A Theology of Liberation*
Edward Said's *Orientalism*
Gayatri Chakravorty Spivak's *Can the Subaltern Speak?*

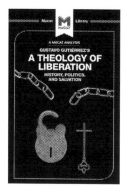

Macat analyses are available from all good bookshops and libraries.

Access hundreds of analyses through one, multimedia tool.
Join free for one month **library.macat.com**

Macat Disciplines

Access the greatest ideas and thinkers across entire disciplines, including

AFRICANA STUDIES

Chinua Achebe's *An Image of Africa: Racism in Conrad's Heart of Darkness*

W. E. B. Du Bois's *The Souls of Black Folk*

Zora Neale Hurston's *Characteristics of Negro Expression*

Martin Luther King Jr.'s *Why We Can't Wait*

Toni Morrison's *Playing in the Dark: Whiteness in the American Literary Imagination*

Macat analyses are available from all good bookshops and libraries.

Access hundreds of analyses through one, multimedia tool.
Join free for one month **library.macat.com**

Macat Disciplines

Access the greatest ideas and thinkers across entire disciplines, including

FEMINISM, GENDER AND QUEER STUDIES

Simone De Beauvoir's
The Second Sex

Michel Foucault's
History of Sexuality

Betty Friedan's
The Feminine Mystique

Saba Mahmood's
*The Politics of Piety:
The Islamic Revival and
the Feminist Subject*

Joan Wallach Scott's
*Gender and the
Politics of History*

Mary Wollstonecraft's
*A Vindication of the
Rights of Woman*

Virginia Woolf's
A Room of One's Own

Judith Butler's
Gender Trouble

Macat analyses are available from all good bookshops and libraries.

Access hundreds of analyses through one, multimedia tool.

Join free for one month **library.macat.com**

Macat Disciplines

Access the greatest ideas and thinkers across entire disciplines, including

CRIMINOLOGY

Michelle Alexander's
*The New Jim Crow:
Mass Incarceration in the
Age of Colorblindness*

**Michael R. Gottfredson
& Travis Hirschi's**
A General Theory of Crime

Elizabeth Loftus's
Eyewitness Testimony

**Richard Herrnstein
& Charles A. Murray's**
*The Bell Curve: Intelligence and
Class Structure in American Life*

Jay Macleod's
*Ain't No Makin' It:
Aspirations and Attainment in a
Low-Income Neighborhood*

Philip Zimbardo's
The Lucifer Effect

Macat analyses are available from all good bookshops and libraries.

Access hundreds of analyses through one, multimedia tool.

Join free for one month **library.macat.com**

Macat Disciplines

Access the greatest ideas and thinkers across entire disciplines, including

INEQUALITY

Ha-Joon Chang's, *Kicking Away the Ladder*

David Graeber's, *Debt: The First 5000 Years*

Robert E. Lucas's, *Why Doesn't Capital Flow from Rich To Poor Countries?*

Thomas Piketty's, *Capital in the Twenty-First Century*

Amartya Sen's, *Inequality Re-Examined*

Mahbub Ul Haq's, *Reflections on Human Development*

Macat analyses are available from all good bookshops and libraries.

Access hundreds of analyses through one, multimedia tool.

Join free for one month **library.macat.com**

Macat Disciplines

Access the greatest ideas and thinkers across entire disciplines, including

GLOBALIZATION

Arjun Appadurai's, *Modernity at Large: Cultural Dimensions of Globalisation*

James Ferguson's, *The Anti-Politics Machine*

Geert Hofstede's, *Culture's Consequences*

Amartya Sen's, *Development as Freedom*

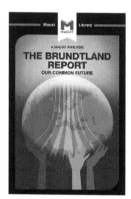

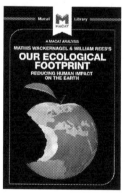

Macat Disciplines

Access the greatest ideas and thinkers across entire disciplines, including

THE FUTURE OF DEMOCRACY

Robert A. Dahl's, *Democracy and Its Critics*
Robert A. Dahl's, *Who Governs?*
Alexis De Toqueville's, *Democracy in America*
Niccolò Machiavelli's, *The Prince*
John Stuart Mill's, *On Liberty*
Robert D. Putnam's, *Bowling Alone*
Jean-Jacques Rousseau's, *The Social Contract*
Henry David Thoreau's, *Civil Disobedience*

Macat Disciplines

Access the greatest ideas and thinkers across entire disciplines, including

TOTALITARIANISM

Sheila Fitzpatrick's, *Everyday Stalinism*
Ian Kershaw's, *The "Hitler Myth"*
Timothy Snyder's, *Bloodlands*

Macat Pairs

Analyse historical and modern issues from opposite sides of an argument. Pairs include:

RACE AND IDENTITY

Zora Neale Hurston's
Characteristics of Negro Expression

Using material collected on anthropological expeditions to the South, Zora Neale Hurston explains how expression in African American culture in the early twentieth century departs from the art of white America. At the time, African American art was often criticized for copying white culture. For Hurston, this criticism misunderstood how art works. European tradition views art as something fixed. But Hurston describes a creative process that is alive, ever-changing, and largely improvisational. She maintains that African American art works through a process called 'mimicry'—where an imitated object or verbal pattern, for example, is reshaped and altered until it becomes something new, novel—and worthy of attention.

Frantz Fanon's
Black Skin, White Masks

Black Skin, White Masks offers a radical analysis of the psychological effects of colonization on the colonized.

Fanon witnessed the effects of colonization first hand both in his birthplace, Martinique, and again later in life when he worked as a psychiatrist in another French colony, Algeria. His text is uncompromising in form and argument. He dissects the dehumanizing effects of colonialism, arguing that it destroys the native sense of identity, forcing people to adapt to an alien set of values—including a core belief that they are inferior. This results in deep psychological trauma.

Fanon's work played a pivotal role in the civil rights movements of the 1960s.

Macat analyses are available from all good bookshops and libraries.

Access hundreds of analyses through one, multimedia tool.
Join free for one month **library.macat.com**

Macat Pairs

Analyse historical and modern issues from opposite sides of an argument. Pairs include:

INTERNATIONAL RELATIONS IN THE 21ST CENTURY

Samuel P. Huntington's
The Clash of Civilisations

In his highly influential 1996 book, Huntington offers a vision of a post-Cold War world in which conflict takes place not between competing ideologies but between cultures. The worst clash, he argues, will be between the Islamic world and the West: the West's arrogance and belief that its culture is a "gift" to the world will come into conflict with Islam's obstinacy and concern that its culture is under attack from a morally decadent "other."

Clash inspired much debate between different political schools of thought. But its greatest impact came in helping define American foreign policy in the wake of the 2001 terrorist attacks in New York and Washington.

Francis Fukuyama's
The End of History and the Last Man

Published in 1992, *The End of History and the Last Man* argues that capitalist democracy is the final destination for all societies. Fukuyama believed democracy triumphed during the Cold War because it lacks the "fundamental contradictions" inherent in communism and satisfies our yearning for freedom and equality. Democracy therefore marks the endpoint in the evolution of ideology, and so the "end of history." There will still be "events," but no fundamental change in ideology.

Macat Pairs

Analyse historical and modern issues from opposite sides of an argument. Pairs include:

MACAT

MACAT

HOW TO RUN AN ECONOMY

John Maynard Keynes's
The General Theory OF Employment, Interest and Money

Classical economics suggests that market economies are self-correcting in times of recession or depression, and tend toward full employment and output. But English economist John Maynard Keynes disagrees.

In his ground-breaking 1936 study *The General Theory*, Keynes argues that traditional economics has misunderstood the causes of unemployment. Employment is not determined by the price of labor; it is directly linked to demand. Keynes believes market economies are by nature unstable, and so require government intervention. Spurred on by the social catastrophe of the Great Depression of the 1930s, he sets out to revolutionize the way the world thinks

Milton Friedman's
The Role of Monetary Policy

Friedman's 1968 paper changed the course of economic theory. In just 17 pages, he demolished existing theory and outlined an effective alternate monetary policy designed to secure 'high employment, stable prices and rapid growth.'

Friedman demonstrated that monetary policy plays a vital role in broader economic stability and argued that economists got their monetary policy wrong in the 1950s and 1960s by misunderstanding the relationship between inflation and unemployment. Previous generations of economists had believed that governments could permanently decrease unemployment by permitting inflation—and vice versa. Friedman's most original contribution was to show that this supposed trade-off is an illusion that only works in the short term.

Macat analyses are available from all good bookshops and libraries.

Access hundreds of analyses through one, multimedia tool.
Join free for one month **library.macat.com**

Macat Pairs

Analyse historical and modern issues from opposite sides of an argument. Pairs include:

ARE WE FUNDAMENTALLY GOOD - OR BAD?

Steven Pinker's
The Better Angels of Our Nature

Stephen Pinker's gloriously optimistic 2011 book argues that, despite humanity's biological tendency toward violence, we are, in fact, less violent today than ever before. To prove his case, Pinker lays out pages of detailed statistical evidence. For him, much of the credit for the decline goes to the eighteenth-century Enlightenment movement, whose ideas of liberty, tolerance, and respect for the value of human life filtered down through society and affected how people thought. That psychological change led to behavioral change—and overall we became more peaceful. Critics countered that humanity could never overcome the biological urge toward violence; others argued that Pinker's statistics were flawed.

Philip Zimbardo's
The Lucifer Effect

Some psychologists believe those who commit cruelty are innately evil. Zimbardo disagrees. In *The Lucifer Effect*, he argues that sometimes good people do evil things simply because of the situations they find themselves in, citing many historical examples to illustrate his point. Zimbardo details his 1971 Stanford prison experiment, where ordinary volunteers playing guards in a mock prison rapidly became abusive. But he also describes the tortures committed by US army personnel in Iraq's Abu Ghraib prison in 2003—and how he himself testified in defence of one of those guards. committed by US army personnel in Iraq's Abu Ghraib prison in 2003—and how he himself testified in defence of one of those guards.

Macat Pairs

Analyse historical and modern issues from opposite sides of an argument. Pairs include:

HOW WE RELATE TO EACH OTHER AND SOCIETY

Jean-Jacques Rousseau's
The Social Contract

Rousseau's famous work sets out the radical concept of the 'social contract': a give-and-take relationship between individual freedom and social order.

If people are free to do as they like, governed only by their own sense of justice, they are also vulnerable to chaos and violence. To avoid this, Rousseau proposes, they should agree to give up some freedom to benefit from the protection of social and political organization. But this deal is only just if societies are led by the collective needs and desires of the people, and able to control the private interests of individuals. For Rousseau, the only legitimate form of government is rule by the people.

Robert D. Putnam's
Bowling Alone

In *Bowling Alone*, Robert Putnam argues that Americans have become disconnected from one another and from the institutions of their common life, and investigates the consequences of this change.

Looking at a range of indicators, from membership in formal organizations to the number of invitations being extended to informal dinner parties, Putnam demonstrates that Americans are interacting less and creating less "social capital" – with potentially disastrous implications for their society.

It would be difficult to overstate the impact of *Bowling Alone*, one of the most frequently cited social science publications of the last half-century.

Macat analyses are available from all good bookshops and libraries.

Access hundreds of analyses through one, multimedia tool.

Join free for one month **library.macat.com**

Printed in the United States
by Baker & Taylor Publisher Services